# He Lives, So Love!

Devotionals for Living the Faith in Every Season

Shirley Henry

**Believer To Book**
**www.believertobook.com**

**He Lives, So Love! / Shirley Henry**
ISBN-13: 978-1945793028
ISBN-10: 1945793023

*I dedicate this book to my earthly father, Van A. Adamson, as one who taught me and showed me his love for me as his daughter. Because of the early morning times of him waking me and taking me out to the garden to share a tomato, and the times he took me hunting rabbits and squirrels—which turned into quietly sitting under a tree, watching the rabbits hop and the squirrels play in the trees—I learned a side of being a daughter that made it easier to know my heavenly Father, the King, and the importance of sharing quiet times with Him. Thank you, Dad, for showing me the importance of time spent in the garden with you, and then with my heavenly Father.*

# CONTENTS

A Note from the Author .................................................. 5

God Comes First

"Because He Lives!" ..................................................... 9

In or On? ................................................................. 13

Respect and Reverence ................................................. 15

"Follow Me" ............................................................ 17

Problems or Opportunities? ........................................... 21

But God! .................................................................. 25

Who Is Your Hero? ..................................................... 29

Love and Grace

Fruit Loops .............................................................. 35

Betrayed ................................................................. 37

Rosebuds ................................................................. 41

Motherhood

Sound Doctrine .......................................................... 47

Love Offers Victory ..................................................... 51

Relax, Relaxing, Relaxed ............................................... 55

Out of Our Prison Cells ................................................ 59

May I Now Retire? ...................................................... 61

Fathers

"Come Sit Awhile" ...................................................69

Our Father's Heart ..................................................73

Honor Thy Father ....................................................77

Glorify His Name ....................................................81


Living Our Faith

Egg Beaters and Can Openers ...............................87

The Man on the Hill ...............................................91

Hunger for the Word ..............................................95

Cross Country .........................................................99

Moses and Aaron ..................................................103

Positive Plus Negative .........................................107

The Hamburger ......................................................111

"Trust Me and Open Your Eyes" ..........................115

Running to Win ......................................................117

Who Says I Am Old? .............................................121


Prayer and Worship

Looking for an Intercessor ....................................127

Whose Shoes Will I Fill? .......................................131

A Knock at the Door ..............................................135

Here I Am, Lord—Send Me! .................................139

Misunderstanding the Woman at the Well .............143

A Spark ..................................................................147

Watch for the Kick ................................................149

Holy Days and Holidays

Call a Solemn Assembly ............................................... 157

God Is Love .................................................................. 161

Play It As It's Written .................................................. 165

Sand or Rock? .............................................................. 169

"Will You Also Go Away?" ........................................... 171

"Come, See a Man" ...................................................... 175

Love Is the Mortar ....................................................... 179

What Does Christmas Mean to Me? .............................. 183

Do I Have a Recipe? ..................................................... 187

365 Days ...................................................................... 193

Time to Huddle ............................................................ 195

Frogs or Freedom? ........................................................ 199


About the Author .......................................................... 204

About Sermon To Book .................................................. 206

# A Note from the Author

Thank you for picking up this copy of *He Lives—So Love!*

The devotionals in this book are written by a mother, grandmother, and wife. But I hope that all of my brothers, sisters, sons, and daughters in Christ may find inspiration, motivation, and renewal in Christ through these written reflections, lessons, scriptures, and prayers the Lord has led me to share with you. This collection of devotions is intended to support your daily walk of faith in any season of the year and any season of life.

There is no rigid plan for reading and praying through these devotional entries. They are grouped into sections by theme, so read them one at a time, all at once, in order, or out of order—however the Spirit leads you!

And may you grow ever closer to the Lord in heart, prayer, and action.

*Shirley Henry*
*Port Washington, Ohio*

# God Comes First

GOD COMES FIRST

# "Because He Lives!"

Years ago I was asked to speak at a women's meeting. I agreed, and my friend and I went. It was a more formal luncheon meeting than I was used to, and there were quite a few people there. Even as I went, I felt very intimidated and was thinking, "What am I doing here? What could I have to say to these women?" I stress that this was not about them; it was about my own struggles with myself.

I was seated next to the woman who was in charge of the meeting. As we were fellowshipping during lunch, she turned to me and asked, "What is your philosophy?" I was shocked and thought, "I don't even know what a philosophy is."

My friend saw I was struggling, and trying to help me, she said, "Shirley has not changed since I met her."

In reply to this, the lady said, "I hope you have grown at least a little bit." Now I was almost in a panic and would have loved to have slid under the table or escaped out the door. But no, it was time for the meeting to start.

I took a deep breath and prayed one of my famous prayers: "Help, Father!"

They had a guest singer who was called upon to begin a time of worship. She took the microphone and began to sing the Bill and Gloria Gather song "Because He Lives!" As she sang, I saw the answer to that simple prayer unfold. In an instant I knew my answer to the lady and every woman there. I knew my philosophy even if I didn't know what that word meant. It was, and still is, *because He lives*: "Because He lives, I can face tomorrow; because He lives all fear is gone; because I know He holds the future and life is worth the living just because He lives."

I don't remember what I spoke about, or anything else of that meeting, but I have never forgotten the answer to her question. That has become my theme song—but more than that, it has become a light to me. That day I had many fears and wasn't sure life was worth living, but when I looked to the fact that He is alive, my life truly changed and I came to the truth that it is all about Him!

Now as an older woman looking at younger women, I want to hold them and tell them this simple truth. He is alive! He cares. He has seen every tear you have cried. But greater still, He holds tomorrow and knows how to walk you through whatever you might be facing. He knows the future; He knows what to do about it and really wants to take you to that place of victory and rest. You see, when He said, "It is finished!" it was finished (John 19:30).

The way has been made for you to go straight to the Father and receive whatever it is you need. The price has been paid—He just needs you to believe and receive it!

GOD COMES FIRST

# In or On?

'In' and 'on'—these are two little words that carry a great big impact on our lives. You see, I believe the Church is full of those who confess to believe *in* God. But do they believe *on* Him?

Can you see the difference? This is how the Holy Spirit taught me:

Years ago I read in the paper about a man who was going to walk across a part of Niagara Falls. It was reported in the newspaper, and the man told how he asked people if they thought he could do it. They were not sure, but then they watched him do it. He afterward came back to those same people and asked them if they now believed he could do it. They clapped for him and said that yes, they now believed it.

Oh, but did they really? His next statement was, "If you believe I can do it, get *on* my back and go with me across." How many of those people do you think got on his back? You are right—not one. That day I saw the difference between believing *in* Jesus and believing *on* Him, I even found a scripture, James 2:19, that says the devils believe *in* Him and tremble.

I began to look at my life and found there were places where I had my 'in' and 'on' backwards. The words 'I believe" came easy, but it wasn't so easy getting my words to "Yes, I will believe *on* You." You see, that meant me getting so close to Him that whatever He said and wherever He went, I would believe He was taking me safely. No way do the devils believe *on* Him, and I am afraid that is true of a lot of people who claim to believe in Him.

Let's check our hearts and see if we will climb on and let Him take us wherever and over whatever He walks. I am learning not to look down or look at the circumstances I can see, but instead to look only to Him and His anointing. I am truly learning to believe *on* Him!

GOD COMES FIRST

# Respect and Reverence

While praying for the Body of Christ today, I was questioning the Father about the lack of commitment I see. As I prayed, the Holy Spirit gave me the word *respect*. He said the problem is a lack of respect for Him and His Word. I almost need to warn us all to stop and think: "Do I really respect Him and His Word?"

I have been teaching on Christ and what He did for us at Calvary. Sometimes my heart breaks because I see and hear us throw around the words like we understand what they say. But do we? Why did He really come? Where did He really bleed? What does it all mean to me? Am I satisfied just to settle for not going to hell, or is there more?

As I ran the references to 'respect' and 'reverence' (which is another meaning of the Hebrew word), I came to Matthew 21:33. Here is the parable of a certain householder who planted a vineyard. When he sent his servants to receive its fruits, the workers beat, killed, and stoned them. So he sent a larger group of servants, but the workers killed them, too. But in verse 37, he sent his son to them, thinking they would at least "reverence" (respect) his son. No—they killed him and looked to seize his inheritance.

So what does that parable say to me? In the old covenant, the Father sent prophets to His people, but the people killed them. So He sent more prophets, who were also killed. We look at these people and wonder, "Why did they do that? We never would have done that—we would have received them gladly and listened to them." Then He sent His very own Son, thinking surely they would receive Him! Do I need to say more?

Have we really received Him in truth, or have we just made up a religion about Him? It says in Matthew 21:45, "they perceived that He spake [spoke] of them" (KJV). Did that change anything? No, they sought to kill Him, too. But as I pray for the Church today I am sorry to say I see the same attitude. We have our own ideas and strategies as to what being a Christian means and our own opinions of how to walk and work for Him.

Maybe we are not physically killing Him, but are we doing what they did and turning our back on Him and everything He did? Are we doing it ourselves, thinking we know better? Where is the respect and reverence?

GOD COMES FIRST

# "Follow Me"

In my studies of our Jewish heritage, I found a teaching by a Messianic rabbi about being a disciple and how they were chosen. He said at the time Jesus was choosing the Twelve, all the young men who were of the age to study under rabbis were chosen by those rabbis while those who were not chosen went on to work for their livelihood. Being chosen was a great honor. It meant the rabbi saw potential in that person—intellect and talents.

The rabbi said that to understand this brings revelation and gives light to a question many, including me, have asked.:Why did Jesus choose who He did, and how could they leave everything at once, including their father's business, without the father going after them? Jesus simply looked at them and said, "Follow Me!"

The twelve Jesus chose were probably those who had been passed over by the other rabbis. As Jesus walked by and said, "Follow Me!" they would have known He was a rabbi and would have been excited to be called. Their father would have been blessed, and because of this he would have rejoiced. His sons were no longer overlooked or rejected!

So as I write this, I believe I sense the heart of our Father as He looks over us. He looks and sees all those who have such a heart to know Him, but when they try to be accepted, they don't fit. Maybe they don't look right, or maybe they don't seem smart enough, or maybe their gifts and talents are a little different. But I say to everyone who feels this way and has walked and is walking outside of what they hunger for on the inside: Jesus is still calling disciples today, and if you look in the Scriptures, He said He came to seek and save those who were lost—lost but so very hungry to be loved. He ate with sinners and was persecuted for it. He found common folk like the woman at the well and revealed Himself to them.

He is passing your way today and His arms are open wide; His eyes are on you, and He is saying, "Follow Me!" Don't be afraid. He is everything you could ever need and oh, how He loves you! You see, He didn't choose by talent, intellect, or position. He chose those who knew they needed Him, those who had been rejected by the establishment. It is recorded in Acts 4:13 that others "marvelled" at the disciples, seeing "they were unlearned and ignorant men" (KJV). But they knew the disciples had been with Jesus. Oh, how we need those who have been with Jesus today!

Finally, I want to share the Hebrew meaning of 'disciple': it is one who follows so close to his teacher that the dust of the teacher's feet gets on them. Today, no matter how unworthy or unlearned we are, may we really know and believe that His eyes are still looking for those who will allow Him to teach them. His arms are outstretched to the hurting, the unlovely, but most of all to those hungry for love and acceptance. He is still saying those same two words to all of us: "Follow Me!" My prayer is that we will answer "yes" and leave all hurts, cares, mistakes, and pride to walk so close to Him that people see the dust from His feet on us!

GOD COMES FIRST

# Problems or Opportunities?

I have learned something that might seem small but has become enormous in my life. I believe it is one of the keys that have been given to us by Jesus. So pay close attention because I want to share it with you and I pray it becomes a blessing to you also.

I had a problem years ago that was so big I didn't know which way to go. I could not go forward, backward, or sideways. Then I read the story of Moses and the children of Israel coming out of the wilderness. The Red Sea was in front of them, the Egyptians behind them. What were they going to do? But Moses cried out to God and He delivered them by parting the sea and letting them go forward on dry ground while drowning their enemy in the very same sea.

I also came across 1 Corinthians 10:11, which says the things that happened to the people of Israel were an example for us of what to do and what not to do. So I took both of the scriptures and my seemingly insurmountable problem to my Father and prayed, "Would you part the sea for me?"

Being in that place of having nowhere to go, I prayed for revelation and a way out of the situation I was in. What a good Father He is—He parted the sea for me and even gave me a revelation to apply to every area of my life! He was so faithful, and I learned about a God who is very real and desires to be real to us. But there are some real decisions to be made.

First, I answered the question of who He is because revelation did come to me. This was a very real Jesus I was talking about and now had to trust. Because when you step into the sea and trust Him to part the waters, it can be scary.

Second, there are keys to this walk, and the one I want to share now is *attitude*.

You see, it is all about attitude and revelation. Matthew 16:15 tells us that Jesus asked Peter, "But whom say ye that I am?" Peter answered, "Thou art the Christ, the Son of the living God" (Matthew 16:16). Jesus told him that flesh and blood had not revealed this to him, but rather His Father in heaven had revealed it to him. And Jesus told the woman at the well, "I that speak unto thee am he [the Christ]" (John 4:26). I was at a place where my Father was saying to me, "Who do *you* say that I am?" I had been in church all my life and knew the stories about what God had done for others, but it came down to what my answer to that question would be. (KJV)

When I face a problem, I have a choice. Will I choose to see it as an opportunity for the Holy Spirit to teach me more about parting the sea, or am I going to see it as a problem that has no solution? When I choose to see it as an opportunity, I can do what He asked me to do and have joy and a heart of thankfulness. It is such an exciting life, and I am so thankful He asked that question of me: "Shirley, who do *you* say that I am?" And I am so thankful that I stepped into the sea!

So my heart today is to ask others the same question. Who do you say that He is, and will you step into the sea and let Him make Himself real to you? Will we as a Church finally let Him be who He is? Will we truly serve and love Him by loving each other and a world that is not very easy to love? I pray our answer today is, "Thou art the Christ, the Son of the living God, and I will follow You wherever You send me!"

GOD COMES FIRST

# But God!

I had friends stay overnight this week, and as we shared I kept hearing myself say over and over, "But God..." I even remarked that if I were ever going to write a book, the title might be *But God*!

As I was thinking about this, I remembered Hap, our first purchase when we bought our farm. He was a beautiful pony. He was one hand from being a horse, but he looked impressive and our kids were so excited to begin riding him. Of course, that just turned into one of those experiences, of which we've had many, of not knowing a thing about what we were doing. As the saying goes, we knew enough to be dangerous!

When they delivered Hap, the owner rode him and showed the kids what he could do. Then the owner left us and we became the new owners of this exciting adventure. The kids couldn't wait to ride Hap! One got on and made it a few feet—then off he went. The second kid got on, and off he went, too. Next came our daughter. Same result!

But we were determined. Next came my husband, and I am sorry to say it, but he experienced the same result as the kids. When my turn came, I was wise enough to say, "That's okay, you guys go ahead and try again."

Well, my brother-in-law and sister-in-law came down to visit and decided they would try. After all, how hard could it be to ride a pony? My sister-in-law got on first and Hap took off! We had a weeping willow tree in our front yard, and Hap headed straight for it. He took her under and around that tree, which I must say was pretty funny. When she came out from under that tree, her wig was hanging on the tree—and yes, we roared, and Hap even jumped for joy.

Now it was getting intense, and my brother-in-law said he would show Hap who was boss. So on he got, and Hap let him ride nicely down the driveway. But it had rained, and there was a puddle there. All at once Hap took off running, and when he came to that puddle, he stopped dead still—and my brother-in-law went right over the top of him, into the puddle. It was like being entertained at a comedy show!

Now everyone left, and my husband looked at Hap. He had had enough, and he was going to be the one to put this comedy to an end. My husband took Hap into a fenced area where there was nothing Hap could do to continue this show. He mounted and Hap took off, right into the fence. He ran so close that my husband was going to be thrown into this barbed wire fence, so he put down one leg to balance himself. Wrong move—Hap took off and my husband landed on the ground with a very injured leg. In fact, he missed six weeks of work. When I called into his work, I told them he had fallen off a pony. When he heard me tell them that, he protested that at least I could have said a horse! I turned my head to hide my face. I would never think of laughing, of course.

We called the former owners, who were good friends, and asked them what was wrong. They had assured us Hap would be great with the kids, so we must be doing something wrong. They came down, and their son got on—and you should have seen Hap. Talk about a show! He pranced and did all kind of fancy moves. When he dismounted, we just looked at him. What was the difference? Then came the answer.

Hap had been trained as a show pony and was trained to respond to the reins against his neck. Can you imagine the signals our family was sending him unintentionally? When we saw how beautiful he could perform, we ensured Hap had a home with a young girl who wanted to show him, while we stuck to dogs and a duck named Donald.

You may be wondering what this has to do with God? How many times do we take hold of a situation, just "knowing" we can handle it when we have not taken the time to let God teach us what we need to know to ride out this situation. He has handled things many times and knows exactly what we need to do with the reins. Maybe, like us, you didn't even know you could train with the reins, so like Israel at the Red Sea with the enemy at their back, it looks like you're done for. *But God!*

As I look back at my life, every time I have faced these kinds of situations. it might have looked like life was going to throw me off, *but God* showed up, took hold of the reins, and taught me how to ride out those situations. You, too, will always be able to say, "But God!"

GOD COMES FIRST

# Who Is Your Hero?

I listen to a rabbi who teaches the meaning of the Hebrew in the Scriptures. This morning he taught me that the word 'hero' is not in the Bible. I checked in my concordance and sure enough, it is not there. I love to study the Scriptures and the true meaning of the words used, so I had to go to the dictionary to find the meaning of 'hero.': it's commonly defined as the main character in a work of fiction. I am sure we have all heard the word used often in sports as well. Our children grow up looking to athletes as their heroes.

This got my mind to running, and I began to think about the people listed in Hebrews 11. It was from this chapter that I had heard teachings about certain people being "the Heroes of Faith." My Bible even heads this chapter with the title "Heroes of Faith".

Now, these people obviously had great faith, so why would the Holy Spirit not use the word 'heroes'? As I thought on this, and asked the Holy Spirit for help and revelation, He brought to my mind what my husband taught our children about playing sports and applying it to life: anytime people or the press make a hero out of you, you had better be grounded in how and why you have done so well at your game that they would even use such a word. There is no one who takes the field or floor to play their game who has not been touched, and is not continuing to be touched, by every other member of that team, the coaches, and the fans who support them. Then you have referees, umpires, cheerleaders, and the parents who sacrifice to get them to practices.

So, what happens to a team when someone thinks they are the "main character" on that team? I can guarantee you, you may make a hero out of yourself, but you will never experience the joy of winning the top rewards as a team. Listen to the quarterback who wins MVP talk to the press. You will hear him say, "It is not all about me, my line did a great job giving me time to throw!"

I think if we look into the lives of these people in Hebrews 11, we will find who the main character or hero was. They failed in certain situations but trusted by their great faith in the real Hero to help them and make a way to victory. Could it be they are listed in this chapter for us to learn from, and not to look to them as heroes? And don't the Scriptures teach us not to think more highly of ourselves than of others? Did Jesus come as a "hero" or as a servant? I believe that in serving, He taught us how to achieve the greater victory. As a team, we who love God reach out to a lost world and win the victory by fulfilling His call!

As pastors and leaders, is it our mindset that what God does must come through us and our denomination, or are we joining with our Hero and becoming one part of His Body that supplies one part of His plan? For example, I wonder who is most important in God's eyes, Billy Graham or the person who led him to Jesus. Is that Sunday school teacher the real hero, or does it go back to a person in the teacher's life?

*Father, help us get it: it is not about "me," it is all about You!* I pray those who claim Jesus as Lord of their life will follow His example and serve one another instead of themselves. There are no heroes in His plan, just examples of His mercy and grace in our lives that cause others to see Him, not to see us as heroes.

## *Notes & Reflections*

_____
_____
_____
_____
_____
_____
_____
_____
_____
_____
_____
_____
_____
_____
_____
_____
_____
_____
_____
_____
_____
_____
_____
_____
_____
_____

# Love and Grace

LOVE AND GRACE

# Fruit Loops

A few years ago, the church I was attending visited another church. At the close of the service, the pastor said, "Every church has a fruit loop." Everyone who was with me turned and looked at me. We had great fun with that on the way home and ever since.

A few weeks later as I thought on this, the Holy Spirit gave me a teaching about fruit loops. First, I began to think about corn flakes. They all look alike, and when you put them in milk, they turn mushy and lose their shape, getting mixed up with the other corn flakes. But fruit loops are different. They have different flavors and different colors. When you put them in milk, they stay exactly who they are. They stay the same color and flavor, and they stay crisp!

Applying this to my life and the Church was easy. We have whole assemblies that try to look alike and act alike. Heaven forbid if we should have any differences of opinions or callings or desires to do certain things out of the ordinary! There is a certain way we must act when we come together to be accepted (or so we think).

But our Father is very different! He has made each of us in our own way, and how His heart must ache when He looks at His people and sees a bunch of mushy cornflakes so far from what He meant us to be! As I thought about it, I realized we even now "sugar-coat" ourselves to make us appear and taste better (or so we think).

I have come away from this time of meditation on fruit loops with such a thankful heart that the Holy Spirit over the years has done such a work in me that I can rejoice over the fact that I am a fruit loop! His Word says He made each one of us unique and very special to Him, so how can He truly fellowship with us if we keep trying to be like someone else?

I have learned to accept myself and am dedicated to finding out who and what that is. I can pray for you also to be and become all He desires for you. I have even found a snack that shows this: you take some fruit loops, M&M's, peanuts, Chex, or any cereal or snack pieces of your choice, and mix and coat them with melted white chocolate. Notice that ingredient will retain its own character, but they're blended into a great-tasting treat!

One final thought: I believe the melted white chocolate that holds everything together is *love*.

*Father, may Your love and the revelation of its power cover us and hold us together, that we might look and taste good to all those we meet. And oh yes—thank You for me becoming a fruit loop, and help me to meet more and more fruit loops among your people! Amen.*

LOVE AND GRACE

# Betrayed

For several weeks, the Holy Spirit has been dealing with me about betrayal. I believe we live in a time of fulfilling the Word found in Luke 21:16, Matthew 24:10, and Mark 13:12, all of which prophesy a time in which family members and neighbors will betray one another. Could it be that we need to prepare ourselves so that we do not become the betrayer, and also know how to deal with being the betrayed one?

As I study, I see a difference between betrayal and denial. Peter denied he knew Jesus, but Judas deliberately sold Him out for money to those that opposed Him. I believe I see the difference. Peter ran to save his life while Judas had a different motive. Judas thought Jesus as the Messiah would set up His kingdom on earth, and when Jesus' plan didn't come together with Judas's plan, Judas became offended, so he betrayed Him.

When I look at myself, I can see how I can be guilty of the same thing, so I am asking the Holy Spirit to reveal any area of my life in which I am betraying Him or others. Do my plans line up with His, or do I have a vision of my own of how His work should be done and His kingdom come? Has He entrusted me with revelation of Jesus but I have turned it around for my own purposes? Can you imagine: Judas walked with Jesus, sat in His presence and heard His words, saw His miracles, and was included in everything the other disciples were a part of—yet because Jesus had a different plan, Judas betrayed Him?

I have had people hurt me by claiming I said things I did not say, telling lies about me and so forth. But I have one experience in which I was betrayed, and there is a great difference. The pain went so deep from that betrayal that I have had to deal with forgiveness many times about that situation.

I had shared my very heart with a person and thought they had shared theirs with me. I completely trusted them. One day I began to sense something was wrong between us, so I asked if I had done something that we needed to straighten out. They said no, and I believed them. Then one night in a group of people, that person broke my confidence and attacked full force. I was so shocked and the pain was so great I couldn't say a thing.

Over the years, I have come to see the motive behind the attack and betrayal. They wanted to do the ministry my husband and I had because in their eyes we were not doing it the way it should be done. And they did do just that. As I sought my Father about all of this, the Holy Spirit gave me the word 'betrayal,' and it has been one of the hardest things I have ever dealt with.

I now know in my spirit we must be prepared in this time because Jesus warned us it would happen. I want to be ready so that I don't do this to anyone and so I am prepared to handle it when it is done to me.

I believe the key word is 'offended.' In the above scriptures, Jesus said they became offended and then betrayed one another. He also said the love of many will become cold, but "he that shall endure to the end ... shall be saved" (Matthew 24:12–13 KJV).

*Holy Spirit, oh how much we need You to reveal the love of the Father and His love manifested in Jesus! Help me to be ready for those who would come to me with my enemies and a kiss, and let me never do the same to anyone else. Amen!*

LOVE AND GRACE

# Rosebuds

While preparing for a children's message about the prodigal son, his brother, and their father at my church, I came across a poem that I received in an email from a friend:

> It is only a tiny rosebud, a flower of God's design. But I cannot unfold the petals with these clumsy hands of mine. The secret of unfolding flowers is not known to such as I God opens this flower so sweetly when in my hands they fade and die. If I cannot unfold a rosebud this flower of God's design, then how can I think I have wisdom to unfold this life of mine? So I'll trust in Him for His leading each moment of every day. I will look to Him for His guidance each step of the pilgrim way. The pathway that lies before me only my Heavenly Father knows. I'll trust Him to unfold the moments just as He unfolds the rose.

This spoke to me of the two sons and the love and care of the father. One son threw away everything but repented and came home to be received with joy as a son not a servant. Perhaps he thought he had all the answers and could take control of his own life, but this led him to a pig pen, eating with the pigs.

The older son, I believe, is the one to study. You see, the younger son came to realize his condition and his broken life, but his older brother seemed to think he had it all together. Could this be the condition of some in the Church? Could we think that doing all those good things should give us more reward than the one who has blown it? And do we wonder how the father could throw the younger son a party, when the older son had stayed with the father and did so much work while his brother was out having a great time?

But maybe our heavenly Father's heart is grieved because He has given us everything yet we really don't want those who haven't been as good to receive such a free gift of mercy and grace. Could the prodigal son really understand more than his older brother that it is all about His grace, not our works?

May the poem about the rosebud speak to our hearts, telling us that we all need to let the Father unfold our lives because it doesn't matter which brother represents us—we all need His mercy and grace to be what He needs us to be.

When I stand before Him, will I start telling Him all the things I have done for Him, or will I know with all my heart the only reason I can stand before Him is the work He did for me? May each of us truly know it is His grace and mercy toward us, and not one thing we have done, that will allow us to stand there in His presence.

## *Notes & Reflections*

# Motherhood

MOTHERHOOD

# Sound Doctrine

One day as I was studying scriptures that apply to women, I turned to Titus 2. I began to read and saw it starts out by telling "the things which become sound doctrine" (Titus 2:1 KJV). Now, I assumed they would be great spiritual things, but I found they were everyday situations I was a part of.

I saw the older women were to "teach the younger women to be sober, to love their husbands, [and] to love their children…" (Titus 2:4 KJV). Then, at the end of these verses, it says to do these things so "that the word of God [would] be not blasphemed" (Titus 2:5). This made me stop and take another look. I certainly didn't want to blaspheme the Word of God!

As I meditated on this scripture, I kept thinking, "How do you teach a young woman to love her husband?" You either love someone or you don't, right? Then the really hard one: "How do you teach them to love their children?" All the mothers I knew loved their children, would have done anything they could to make sure their children had everything they needed, and would have done anything to protect them. So, what was this about teaching them to love?

It didn't take long for me to begin to see that a mother's love without understanding can be a very dangerous thing. There were times I thought discipline was a little too hard, not only at home but by teachers or anyone else who even dared correct my children. I wanted to baby them. After all, they are just little kids and they are so cute and oh, how those big eyes can look into yours with an innocent look! They almost shout, "Help, Mom!"

When they got older and played sports, I wanted them to do so well that I found myself praying, "Oh God, help them win!" Then one night at a game while praying my famous prayer, I realized there were twelve moms on the other team wanting their boys (or girls) to win. My mother's heart had a hard time, but I finally let go and cheered for them to do their very best. After all, how did I expect God to choose which mother's prayer He was going to answer?

Now it was time to see what God said about loving your children. He said in Proverbs 3:12 that He corrects the people He loves and that this is a sign of Him being our loving Father. I knew this would not be mean discipline, but discipline that prepared us to be blessed by Him and know His love. Next I found 1 Corinthians 13, which describes in detail what His love looks like, and I knew for us as mothers to love like that, we would have to be taught.

So now, as an older woman, I would say to you young mothers: relax, enjoy, correct, but know that the dirt on your floor from little feet will someday be precious to you. A perfectly clean home in no way compares to the laughter that comes from that child. We had a rule in my home after I studied these scriptures: "We are going to have fun whether anyone wants to or not!" No pouting, no complaining. Let's enjoy every day!

The following is a story I love about two boys:

Two little boys, ages eight and ten, were excessively mischievous. They were always getting into trouble. and their parents knew all about it. If any mischief occurred in their town, the two boys were probably involved.

The boy's mother heard that a preacher in town had been successful in disciplining children, so she asked if he would speak with her boys. The preacher agreed, but he asked to see them individually.

So the mother sent the eight-year-old first, in the morning, and sent the older boy to see the preacher in the afternoon.

The preacher, a huge man with a deep booming voice, sat the younger boy down and asked him sternly, "Do you know where God is, son?"

The boy's mouth dropped open, but he made no response, sitting there wide-eyed with his mouth hanging open.

So the preacher repeated the question in an even sterner tone, "Where is God?"

Again, the boy made no attempt to answer.

The preacher raised his voice even more and shook his finger in the boy's face and bellowed, "Where is God?"

The boy screamed and bolted from the room, ran directly home and dove into his closet, slamming the door behind him.

When his older brother found him in the closet, he asked, "What happened?"

The younger brother, gasping for breath, replied, "We are in *big* trouble this time!

"God is missing and they think *we* did it!"

Children are so real! Let's enjoy and bless them! Again, let's discipline as our Father does us because we love our children, but let's also make sure we understand what loving discipline is and enjoy every stage they go through.

MOTHERHOOD

# Love Offers Victory

This morning my heart is with the young mothers who are looking ahead at school starting. I remember well those days, but I was never bombarded like they are today. Ads have already started on TV as to the school clothes they must have. Lists have been given to stores for the supplies that they must purchase. And then there are always the famous words, "But Mom, all the kids are getting this kind!"

One day years ago while studying my Bible, I read the well-known scripture in which Jesus gives us His second commandment: "...Thou shalt love thy neighbor as thyself" (Matthew 22:39 KJV). But this day as I read it, I looked out my window at my neighbor's house and I had this thought: "If I love Margaret like I love myself, Margaret is in big trouble."

This commandment began to be at the root of all my study. What did it even mean to love myself? I shared this with my husband, and one day he brought to me what the Holy Spirit had shown him. He had taken the word 'love' and written it like this:

L ove
   O ffers
      V ictory
         E verytime to everyone!

Okay, I had it: love is the key to victory. But how did I apply it to myself? I had known people who were in love with themselves, and had been guilty of this myself when I was religious. I didn't ever want to go back there, so there had to be a simple answer. As usual, when we have revelation of the Scriptures that seems so hard to understand, it really is very simple. This is my message to all the grandmas, mothers, and daughters today: love yourself!

You see, first I must be grounded in the fact that God loves *me*, not just *us*. I must see it personally. How would you feel if you had created something and it had the power to be that thing or to refuse to be it, and always tried to be something else? Well, that is how I began to see myself. If I believe Scripture, and that my heavenly Father, who is Creator of the whole universe, formed me in my mother's womb, then what does it do to His heart when He sees me try to be what others are and to do what they do?

When I accept myself as He made me, I can accept the fact that He also made you. As I allow myself to become just what He wanted me to be and do, then I can allow you the same privilege. How can I love you when I don't even like who I am? And we really don't believe God loves us if we don't see how much love He put into practice when He formed us. So a word, especially to all the mothers who are looking at "back to school": Remember God loves you and knows what you need and how to get it to you. Don't let advertisements and what other mothers are doing and buying control you.

Could we just take this time to ask our Father what He has placed in us, and become it? Could we look at our children and teach them they don't have to have the exact thing that "everyone" has or wears, but that they are so special to God and you that you want them to have the courage to become who they are? Yes, there are times when it feels good to have what someone else has, but how much better it feels when you get comfortable with who you are!

I look forward to every member of the Body of Christ becoming and loving themselves as God made them. Can you even imagine the power that would be released into the world if we all were to love ourselves and then love others in the same way? Jesus said it like this: "This is My commandment, That ye love one another, as I have loved you" (John 15:12 KJV).

Now I see, the God we serve is love, and His Son accepted that love and became and did exactly what the Father said and did. And now it is my place to accept who I am in Him, to know His love for me, and to become and do exactly what I was created to be and do. Yes, His love *offers* victory every time to everyone, but I must *accept* it and believe He loves me, especially by being comfortable with—and loving—how He made me!

MOTHERHOOD

# Relax, Relaxing, Relaxed

'Relax'—what an interesting word!

As I look at that word in the three forms—'relax,' 'relaxing,' 'relaxed'—I realize I started out knowing I had to *relax*.

I wasn't sure how to do it, however, so I started practicing *relaxing*. My goal was to go to the last form and live my life *relaxed*.

I did pretty well when my four children were of elementary-school age. We went camping every weekend. There was a river or lake to sit by, a campfire, and s'mores, marshmallows, and hotdogs roasted over that fire.

Then the weekends became ballgames, practices, traveling, and uniforms to have washed and ready. The word 'relax' was now becoming a learning process. I was headed to understanding living while relaxing.

I took a deep breath and found that special place where I could leave the hustle and bustle. For me, it became my porch swing on my back porch. It was the time in the morning after my husband left for work and before my children got up.

I had so much to learn about knowing what I needed to do and knowing how to do it. I tried very hard but found it was not so easy when things happened. Things like my daughter coming in the house with a piece of twig stuck in her eyeball, saying she thought she had something in her eye. 'Relaxing' was a word that seemed far away from me at this time of my life.

Then one day while sitting on my swing, I read in my Bible I was to cast all my care on Jesus. That sounded good, so I tried and tried, but the care was still there. But one day, the word 'cast' stood out to me. I saw myself casting my care like a fisherman casting his line out. There was my problem: like the fisherman, I kept casting but I also kept reeling it back in—with a husband, four children, a farm, coaches, everyday tasks, pressure and more pressure to just hold things together how could I ever find time to be relaxing.

Then came the word 'relaxed.' For as I kept casting the cares of my life onto Him, I realized, somewhere along the way, a new word had come into my life The word 'rest' had become my way to being relaxed. I saw Jesus wanted me to rest in the fact that when I cast my cares, pressures, decisions, and yes, my whole life on Him and leave it there, I entered a place called His rest.

This became a lifesaving event, as I learned I had started out knowing I need to relax, learning how to be relaxing, and finally learning to live relaxed.

Resting in Him brought all the cares and worries into precious memories because I learned to see beyond those cares and worries to the joy of having a husband, four children, and all the activities they brought.

I am so thankful for the time on the porch swing because it helped me realize I had to learn to cast and not reel back in. I am thankful for the time spent practicing casting because it led me to resting in Jesus, which was the key to living relaxed. What an experience to go from *relax*, to *relaxing*, to *relaxed*. I am so thankful for that experience because now I can live relaxed and enjoy all the memories that bring joy and not regrets.

MOTHERHOOD

# Out of Our Prison Cells

On my heart this year are women—women who have listened to all the false teachings they have heard over the years in the media and press, telling them all that they should be and do. I look in my heart and see them in prison cells, not in real prisons but in prisons of their own making. When I look closely, I see the cell doors are unlocked but the women are afraid to come out. There are guards in the halls that represent fear, insecurity, lies, and manipulation. My heart cries out: Is there no one who will go in and bring them out? Are there some older women who will obey the Scriptures and teach the younger how to walk out their roles as wives and mothers? Are there some older women who will take time to pray and hear the heart of our Father as He weeps for those in prison cells?

So grandmas, I guess (no, I *know*) I would like to give you that assignment. Let's hear His heart and intercede for these women. Let's be willing to go wherever He sends us—to share the Word, His love, and His mercy with them. To pray they see they cannot do all things the world tells them, only what the Father has lined up in His Word. To show them the prison cell doors are not locked, they just need to confront those guards, who would like to keep them there, and put their eyes on Jesus, who has the keys to those cell doors. In fact, He has already unlocked them, and if they will decide to come out, He sends His Holy Spirit to lead them out of the prison!

So grandmas, I believe first we must make sure we have not bought any of the enemy's lies, take a look at our own lives to see if we live in His freedom, and then *go in after them*. This year I have been studying the woman who was bowed over when Jesus said to the religious leaders, "And ought not this woman, being a daughter of Abraham, whom Satan hath bound, be loosed...?" (Luke 13:16 KJV). If we belong to Jesus, we too are the seed of Abraham through Him, and so I declare and cry out to Him on behalf of the women in the Body of Christ: Yes! *Yes* ! *YES*!

MOTHERHOOD

# May I Now Retire?

May I pour out my heart this month as a seventy-seven-year-old mom? For the past few weeks I have been asking this question. Is there a time when I can retire from the heart of being a mom? You see, I have had four children who are all very different—may I stress the word *very*?—and yes, they all are exactly who they are. As I look back, I can see that the learning and the joy that have taken place are amazing, and yet the tears and heartbreak are beyond anything I can write here. What is this thing called motherhood, and what did God have in mind when He placed it inside of us? How would I ever describe it?

I think I should have known something was up when I held that tiny baby in my arms and immediately forgot the pain I had in bringing that baby into the world. Only God could bring that about. How could I ever imagine the feeling I would experience when I was correcting that child and they looked up at me with that look in their eyes, and with tears running down those chubby cheeks said, "I love you Mommy"? Then would come the dandelion flower as a love token for me. Who would have ever thought I would place that dandelion in water and try to save it as long as I could?

I remember the pain as I stood by the graveside of my two-year-old daughter Diane and heard the screams coming out of my very being, but I also remember the love of my heavenly Father as one day He healed that broken heart.

I remember the time my daughter Jamie came in and said she had something in her eye, and when I looked there was a twig sticking out of her eyeball. We ran to the eye doctor and found out if it had been just a little deeper, or if I had tried to pull it out, the fluid would have run out of her eye. Again I was reminded of my thankfulness to my Father.

I have sat in a room with seven specialists and heard them tell my husband and I that they had no idea what was wrong or what to do about the symptoms of my daughter Jan, herself now two years old. Then they asked us to decide what we wanted them to do. They could experiment with surgeries or just wait and see what happened. We went back to the Father, who led us to feel we should wait, and the specialists agreed. Today, forty years later, that daughter has given me a great blessing in a now nine-year-old grandson.

I have done all the things mothers of athletes do, like washing uniforms, taking kids to practices and picking them up, having three suppers an evening, and so forth. I have known the joy of seeing one of my sons win a state championship in basketball. But what I experienced as a mother during that season, there are no words to express. It would start with the playing of the National Anthem down in my stomach. I wanted so much for him to do well and for the team to win that I couldn't really tell you what went on during the game, only the feeling of a mother turning her child over to a coach and the screaming of a crowd and the opponents who wanted to stop him at any second. Somewhere along the way, though, I realized there was a mother on the other side who was going through the same thing, and then I just gave the whole thing over to my Father.

I have recently watched another son receive news no mother wants to hear. In an instant I wanted to scoop that grown son up and cradle him in my arms and make the hurt go away with a kiss and a hug as I would have done when he was little. And then I remembered the time he almost cut his thumb off in the fourth grade, when he fell on cinders. I took him to the doctor, who asked me if I could stand the sight of blood. I said "sure" and held my son's hand so the doctor could stitch him up. What I didn't realize was that the doctor had to scrub it first with a brush to get all the cinders out, and I had to hold the thumb open from his hand. Again that mother heart from my Father kicked in, and I did it—no, that is not true: my Father did it, for which I am so thankful.

Now they are all grown up with grandchildren of their own, which makes me a great-grandmother, and my mother heart is still beating. The problem is I have had to learn even more to trust and rely on my Father because I can no longer kiss and make their hurt go away. But as I sometimes think that I would like to retire from motherhood, I find myself simply adjusting and turning to the memories I have. You see, every time I needed Him, He was there. And the joys of motherhood far outweigh the negative, for He turned every negative into a positive.

## *Notes & Reflections*

_____

_____

_____

_____

_____

_____

_____

_____

_____

_____

_____

_____

_____

_____

_____

_____

_____

_____

_____

_____

_____

_____

_____

_____

_____

# Fathers

FATHERS

# "Come Sit Awhile"

Every year when Father's Day approaches, we rush around finding a gift and preparing a meal especially for him. This is all well and good, but I hear the cry of my heavenly Father's heart, and if my dad were here today they would both say the same thing: "Shirley, forget all the hassle and come sit awhile with me."

You see, in prayer recently, I have heard that in my heart. I hear our Father's cry for us to lay aside anything that keeps us from just sitting with Him—sitting without watching the clock or thinking about all we need to be doing.

As I thought about this, I remembered those special times with my dad. We would go early in the morning into our garden with a salt shaker and pick and eat a fresh tomato right there at the edge of the garden. He would take me hunting for rabbits or squirrels. We would sit down under a tree, and he would say, "Be very quiet!" There we sat watching the rabbits and squirrels play while he held his gun, never even aiming it or shooting it one time. What an example he was of my heavenly Father. So now when I hear Josh Groban sing, "Come sit awhile with Me," in his song "You Raise Me Up," it is easy for me to follow my dad's example and just sit and enjoy everything my Father is teaching me about Himself.

When is the last time you sat down and admired His creation, telling Him how beautiful and wonderful it is? When is the last time you read the Scriptures and fellowshipped with Him by asking what He meant when He said those things?

I was taking my eight-year-old grandson somewhere and tried to carry on a conversation, I only heard quick replies, so I looked over at him. There he was with a cell phone, playing a game or texting. I told him that we were going to put that away and share what we were doing at school and home. He agreed, and we had fun learning about each other's day. Now, I know I am being a grandma here, but I look around everywhere I go and there most people are, a cell phone at their ear or in their hands as they text.

All of this leads me to think of Martha and Mary. Martha was rushing around doing things and Mary was sitting at the feet of Jesus. When Martha got upset, Jesus answered with these words: "But one thing is needful, and Mary hath chosen that [thing]…" (Luke 10:42 KJV).

I wonder how seriously we take Him when He says "*one* thing" and we see it is a choice. What if doing that one thing took care of all our needs? Wouldn't you think we would take it seriously and do it. So this Father's

Day, let's say to our dads, grandfathers, and especially our heavenly Father, "I want to come sit awhile with You!"

FATHERS

# Our Father's Heart

Every Father's Day, I pray about what would be pleasing to my Father this year. My own father has gone on to the presence of the Lord, and I have many good memories of him, for which I am very thankful. But how about my heavenly Father? Are memories from a long time ago all I have of Him, or am I still aware of His goodness right now? You see, as I look back at my life, I realize I have walked through many situations, and at the end of those experiences one thing was always present— His love. I came to know a father's love in my Father's care and love for me.

When I moved into my present home, I made one bedroom a little girl's room complete with collectible dolls and teddy bears. It was in there I found the comfort to go on from the loss of my husband. It was in there I learned it was so pleasing to my Father for me to come to Him as a little girl. At that time I learned a song, written by Jeanne Johnson, that says, "Hold me." I sang it many times, as I had decisions to make all alone now that my husband and I would have made together. I learned what it meant to crawl up on His lap and let Him love the hurt away. But during that time I also learned that His heart longs for all of His children to crawl up there and get to know Him, not only as God but also as a Father.

As I studied the Scriptures, I realized that in all of the Old Testament His people were called "children of God." But when Jesus came, He introduced Him as "My Father" and also told us to pray to Him as "our Father." In my study I came to realize this is why the religious leaders got so angry at Him. Who did He think He was to call God "Father"? This was blasphemy in their eyes. After all, they were the way into the Holy of Holies; they were the men you brought your sacrifices to, and they knew all the things necessary to become "holy" or spiritual enough to enter in there.

So, what was this man Jesus saying? They asked Him, "Are you telling the people they can know this Father and talk to Him themselves? Are you saying this is why you came? Do you really believe your message that the kingdom of God is at hand and available to everyone, not just the priest? Why, you even healed people on the Sabbath! You broke our traditions of worship, and now the people are believing and following you! They have even begun to say that surely you are the Son of God. What is this—a Son and not just a child?"

As I studied, I saw the Father's heart. He loves us so much, He longs to be our Father in all senses of that word. He only asks that we honor and obey Him and that we come to Him through the work and obedience of His Son. Can we grasp that Jesus only said the things His Father said to say and only did the things His Father said to do? Can we grasp that Jesus did the work for us to enter straight into the Holy of Holies and into our Father's presence? Yet it was not just for us alone, but for whoever will come. Time spent in the presence of our Father thus gives us the heart needed to love others.

This Father's Day, may we make it a day to honor our heavenly Father and not just earthly fathers. Let's make it a day to loose His love on everyone we meet. Let's believe them to be no longer only the collective 'children of God,' but through a relationship with Jesus to be His sons and daughters. Let's open our hearts to the rest of His family in honor of Him. Let's study His Word and take seriously what He says and how He says to do it.

Years ago, I was asked to play the piano for a summer Bible school at a church I did not attend. Once, at the closing of the day, the pastor asked what any of the children had learned. One little boy, maybe seven or eight, held his hand up so excited and the pastor asked him what he had learned. The little boy said with a big smile, "Jesus loves me!" The pastor looked at him and said, "No, I mean something important!" I will never forget the look on that little boy's face. He was so hurt, but no more than I was.

I have prayed many times over the years for that little boy because I believe there is no more important lesson learned than that "Jesus loves me," and so does my Father. Let's honor Him this Father's Day—but also every day!

FATHERS

# Honor Thy Father

A few days ago, my five-year-old grandson and his uncle were fishing in our little pond all afternoon. It was a fun time, and they had caught about twenty-one small fish. He was very excited but also tired. They came in to eat some supper and take a break. He looked exhausted and I thought surely he must be hungry. I asked him if he was hungry, and he hesitated a bit and then said "no." Uncle John asked, "Are you sure you don't want a hotdog?" Now, he really likes hotdogs, so when he said "no" again after more thought, I knew something was going on. I then said "Are you sure?" to which he replied, "If I eat one, could we not call it supper, because I am supposed to go home to eat supper?" My son and I had to laugh, but later on the Holy Spirit came to teach me through this situation.

I began to think about Preston honoring what his parents had told him. Of course, then my thoughts went to myself and honoring my own father. I looked at how

Preston had tried to get around what they had said in order to do what he really wanted to do, and I could readily see the many times I had done the same thing with rules put in place by my parents. But now, in celebrating Father's Day, maybe it's time to look at our heavenly Father and the things He has told us to do or not to do.

First let's look at why He even says there are some things we should not do. Is it because He wants to have control of us and what we do? Is He a mean God, or could it be because He sees something we don't see, something that would hurt us and His purposes for our life? Could it be that He loves each of us so much that He wants us to believe in His goodness and His grace to bring every good and perfect gift to us?

Next, let's look at the word 'honor.' In the Greek of the New Testament, it means "to prize, to fix a valuation upon, to revere, to esteem to the highest degree and dignity itself."

The next step is to meditate on those definitions. Do those words truly describe my attitude towards my heavenly Father? Do I really hold Him in that place, or like Preston am I looking for a way around what He thinks and says to me in His Word—so I can have what I really want, even if He said "no" to that thing or behavior?

I began to think back to the time when my grandparents lived with us. When my grandfather came into the room, we stood and gave him first place in what was happening in that room. When the table was set for a meal, he sat at the head of the table and we all knew he was the head of this family. When he passed away, my dad took his place at the head of the table. Maybe this sounds strange to you but it has taught me much about honoring my heavenly Father. When I got married and had family gatherings of both sides of the family, I placed my dad at the head, but he came to me and said that I should sit my husband's dad in that place and my husband would sit to his side.

What a teaching I received from all of this! The Word says Jesus is the Head of the Church, so do I have Him seated at the head of my spiritual and physical table? Since my heavenly Father has seated Him at His right hand in a place of authority, have I seated myself there in Him, or have I just tried to seat myself there without Him? Does what He says in the Word settle everything for me, or do I think of how I can change the wording as my grandson did with the word 'supper' so I can do what I actually want to do? Maybe we could call it a snack! Wouldn't that make it alright? No, I don't believe so. Let's call it what it is!

You see, it was very easy to fix my grandson's situation. I told him he must tell the truth and grandma would not lie for him. So the next step was to call his mommy and daddy and ask if it was alright this time to have supper at Grandma's with Uncle John. It was, and I pray that Preston and all of us absorb the revelation that truth always brings blessings, even if it hurts for a season.

We need to be on the lookout for this attitude of working out a way to get what we want even if our Father says otherwise:

Instead of saying, "Let no corrupt communication proceed out of your mouth, but that which is good to the use of edifying, that it may minister grace unto the hearers" (Ephesians 4:29 KJV), we might reason, "What I am saying is not corrupt; it is just me wanting to help the situation." But is it ministering grace and edifying the people hearing it, or could it be bringing division?

How about Ephesians 4:31–32—"Let all bitterness, and wrath, and anger, and clamour, and evil speaking, be put away from you, with all malice: And be ye kind one to another, tenderhearted, forgiving one another, even as God for Christ's sake hath forgiven you" (KJV)? I will let you come up with how we change the words there.

These scriptures are like 'supper' in my story, and 'snack' is like what we change God's Word to say so we can do what we want to do. But can you see, when we should be having a feast of blessing by honoring our Father and how He said to do it, we can't be willing to settle for a snack? May this Father's Day truly be a time of honoring our Father and His ways!

FATHERS

# Glorify His Name

I attended a meeting this week called "Rejoice," where we were singing the song "Glorify Thy Name" by Benny Hinn, and a word was given from the heart of our Father. He said He wants to glorify His name and His Son, but to do that we must love one another. John 15:8 says, "Herein is my Father glorified, that you bear much fruit" (KJV). The key is that before and after this verse, we are told by Jesus to abide in Him who *is* love.

We have been told to love our neighbor as ourselves, but here in John 15:12 we are given a new commandment. Jesus tells us to "love one another, as I have loved you" (KJV). This is an entirely different thing. It is one thing to love others as we love ourselves and another to love one another as He has loved us. If we look at the chapters surrounding this verse, we see these are the last words given to His disciples before being arrested. I believe that makes these words of the utmost importance.

Let's look at John 13:34, where we hear the same thing again; but this time He adds, in verse 35, "By this shall all men know that ye are my disciples, if ye have love one to another" (KJV). And then there is 1 John 4:20: "If a man say, I love God, and hateth his brother, he is a liar: for he that loveth not his brother whom he hath seen, wow can he love God whom he hath not seen?" (KJV).

I guess what I am trying to say this Father's Day is that it is time to look at ourselves and judge by the words of Jesus. We say we belong to Him and call God our Father, but where is the *honor* and where is the obedience? Where is the love?

At that same meeting I attended, the speaker used a scripture in Ezekiel that speaks to my heart because I believe it is a cry from our Father's heart:

> *...the children of thy people still are talking against thee by the walls and in the doors of the houses, and speak one to another, every one to his brother, saying, Come, I pray you and hear what is the word that cometh forth from the LORD. And they come unto thee as my people cometh, and they sit before thee as my people, and they hear thy words, but they will not do them: for with their mouth they shew much love, but their heart goeth after their covetousness. And lo, thou art unto them as a very lovely song of one that hath a pleasant voice, and can play well on an instrument, for they hear thy words, but **they do them not**. — Ezekiel 33:30–32 (KJV, emphasis added)*

You see, we sing praises to our Father, we hear good speakers, we talk to each other about how good the meeting was and how the speaker was great. Then we forget to leave the meeting and do what they said from the Word, and our praise turns to grumbling and gossip. Again, where is the love?

If I have to stand before our Father and be judged upon 1 John 4:20, what will He say when I tell Him that I love Him and He judges my love for Him by how I loved you? *Father, please help us, and may we receive grace and forgiveness.*

# Notes & Reflections

_____

_____

_____

_____

_____

_____

_____

_____

_____

_____

_____

_____

_____

_____

_____

_____

_____

_____

_____

_____

_____

_____

# Living Our Faith

LIVING OUR FAITH

# Egg Beaters and Can Openers

When our youngest children were very small, my friend and I were talking on the phone. At that time, we were doing a study at church called the "Housewife Special." Our pastor was stressing that according to James 1:22, we were to be "doers of the Word and not hearers only" (KJV). It was a good study, and we both were into it with everything we had. So as we shared with one another, we were trying to find out how to do all these things we were reading in the Bible. This can be a real adventure, especially in the beginning of your walk as a "doer."

As we were sharing on this day, my friend began to laugh, and then came a picture and understanding of how we must have looked to our Father. She said her two-year-old son, who evidently was hungry for lunch, was sitting on the floor with an egg beater trying to open a can of soup. I got the picture, and we had a good laugh. We could see our Father looking at us saying, "Girls,

girls what are you doing? You have the right heart to want to learn, you are hungry for My ways, but you are using all the wrong ways of opening it up to you." He needed a can opener, not an egg beater and we needed to learn that our Father has the right tools to open up the revelation of His Word so we can do it in a way that is pleasing to Him.

I believe the first lesson we had to learn came when I went to the county fair with her. Her daughter was entering in a contest, and I was looking around while she was doing what she had to do. I came across the neatest display of Holly Hobbie dolls that people had painted. I enjoy dolls, so I was looking them over and found my favorite one. It was beautiful! Her dress was painted plain pink (in fact the whole doll was plain) and was done just the way I would have done it.

Well, my friend came to the display, and I couldn't wait to show her this beautiful doll I had found. But she took one look at it and said, "Oh, this other one is done much better. It has different colors of plaid painted on it; it is much nicer than that plain pink one."

I didn't say anything then, but when I got home I felt so dumb. I kept asking myself how I could be so wrong—how I didn't even know my doll was not beautiful yet she knew which one was. I lived with this feeling in every area of my life at that time.

But somewhere in the course of studying the Word to be a doer, I found that my Father loved me and had formed me in my mother's womb. It was His intent that we be different and like different things. When I realized this truth, I shared my struggle with my friend. The way the comments about the dolls affected me was a real surprise to her. But we learned through the Holly Hobbie doll that we were going to be walking this walk of being a doer in different ways and we had to learn to accept each other and how the Holy Spirit led each of us.

Today as I walk with the Body of Christ, I see the same thing happening: "If I like green, you should too. If I pray an hour a day, you should too."

When I was in Africa, I had a very real experience that I cannot forget. I was asked to pray for the women in the meeting, and with much care, all I could do was trust my Father to help me. Well, there were probably twenty-five women who came forward. They did not stand before me but knelt down. I started at one end and went to the other end, but to my surprise not one woman had moved from her kneeling position until I had prayed for all of them. I was so humbled by this and said so to the pastor, for you see, the floor they were kneeling on was dirt—or so I thought. What he proceeded to tell me was that the floor was manure.

I will never be the same. I saw so much unity and hunger for Christ, and they didn't want it all for themselves but knelt until all had received.

My prayer for the Church is that we will learn if we are going to be "doers" of His Word, we are going to have to learn we do not do things with our own choice of tools, but instead must learn to accept ourselves and then accept others as they are. You see, it is easy to quote the second commandment of Jesus: "Thou shalt love thy neighbor as thyself" (Matthew 22:39 KJV). But if you really look at that commandment and allow the Holy

Spirit to teach and give you the right tools to obey it, you can only love your neighbor to the extent that you have accepted who He made you to be and love what He has given you to do.

*Father, help me to use the right equipment at the right time. May even my words become a tool in Your hands. Amen!*

# The Man on the Hill

When I awoke this morning, I remembered an incident that happened many years ago to my youngest son and his friends. But as I thought about it, it took on new meaning.

He had asked to have a campout with some of his friends. This was nothing new, and plans were made. It was going to be in our barn, and kids were invited.

My husband was working afternoons, so I was "in charge." That's where the fun started. We had a pond that was treated so they could swim, fish, play ball, and whatever else middle school boys do when they camp out.

I settled in for a nice evening when they came running in, excited and fearful. This is where the evening became not just a campout but a very real adventure. It was now dark, and they told me there was a man on the hill who had built a fire and was walking around it and then bedded down. I went to the window and sure enough, there he was. I could see him in the light of his fire.

So, as a good mom, I took charge: I placed each boy at a window to keep watch until my husband got home. I went from window to window to see what they were seeing and to keep an eye on this man. We lived just over the hill from Interstate 77, so I thought it could be someone who was taking a rest from his travels. I can't remember all the stories, but the boys got excited about this experience and their imaginations went wild.

Now, this went on for several hours because my husband didn't get home until about 12:30 a.m. Finally we saw him pull in, and I went running with the news that a man was camped out on our hill. He could see the fire and this man sleeping beside it, so he told all the boys to stay in the house. He got his shotgun, of all things, and headed up the hill.

Later he told us the rest of the story. When he got there with his gun in hand, he kicked the man and asked him what he was doing. You can imagine the surprise and terror for someone to wake up to a man standing over you with a gun!

But the next thing I saw was my husband walking down the hill with this man and all at once he didn't look so big. It was a neighbor boy who had not gotten invited to my son's campout and had just wanted to be a part of it. When the boys saw who it was, they embraced him, and now the real campout began in the barn.

It had not been intentional, but he had been left out. As I began to think about this today, I wondered how many times someone has built a fire within my sight, and even came and camped there. How many times have I not included a person in my walk with Jesus because I was afraid and I had a picture of what I thought about them? They were different and I didn't know why they were there. Would they think I wouldn't want to be their friend? After all, I didn't invite them into the fellowship of my other friends. Could it be that I just didn't stop and think about the one who simply wanted to be included in what looked like something great, but wasn't invited?

As the Body of Christ, may we look—really look—at ourselves and ask, "Have we become so comfortable with our own little 'party' that we don't invite others to it?"

*Father, help us see and include "the man on the hill" in our lives and invite them to Your party! Amen!*

LIVING OUR FAITH

# Hunger for the Word

After attending Sunday school classes this morning, I feel as if my heart is breaking for the Body of Christ! We are studying 2 Timothy 2:15: "Study to shew [show] thyself approved unto God, a workman that needeth not to be ashamed, rightly dividing the word of truth" (KJV).

It reminded me of my time in Africa. I was teaching a group of women and pastors when I made a statement to the effect that they should get in the Word and study. When the meeting was over, the pastor who I was traveling with came to me and said, 'Do you know that not one woman here, or the pastor, has a Bible?" I was shocked! That thought never crossed my mind. Doesn't every one in the Church have one?

I thought about my own library of books. When I got home, I found I had five Bibles plus concordances and commentaries. I reflected on how easily and quickly we can give someone good advice or true instruction, yet they have no way of doing it. So, what is my part?

I went to the pastor who was overseeing my visit and asked him what I could do. He told me, and every woman there received their Bible, the pastor included.

I have never forgotten or gotten over that experience. So now when I begin to study as the Scriptures say I should, I remember those women and their hunger to learn though they had no Bible to study. The challenge for me was deciding what I should do once I knew that situation existed. Would I just forget (or try to) or once I knew, did the Father expect me to do something?

We asked ourselves that question today in our class. I have asked myself that question many times. What do I do, and how do I do it? You see, I was a very religious person. I had a Bible but never studied it with the intention of doing what it said. I sometimes spent time in devotions, but after my experience of receiving Jesus as my everything, I found study to be entirely different from devotions.

I also know that I can't get caught up in wanting everyone to catch my heart for Africa, or in just doing good works. What I am saying then, Body of Christ, is to please hear what your Father is saying to you to do, and to carry it in your heart in prayer. Jesus is the Head of the Church, so I am sure He has a plan that meets every need of every person whether they are in Africa or Tuscarawas County, Ohio. How about that little boy down the road? How about that friend in the nursing home? It is so easy to talk about what we should do, or better yet what the other person should be doing.

I was asked one time what the most important lesson I had learned as a Christian was. I had to think a moment, but then I knew. Besides learning what Jesus has done for me, the most important lesson I have learned is, "There is always a 'rest of the story'!" We judge so quickly, but if we know the other part of the story, judging goes out the window.

So before we speak too quickly to tell others what they should be doing, we need to hear where they are at and what they have been through. You see, in Africa I just taught as I would have here, where every woman coming to the meeting would have had a Bible. But today my heart is breaking because who is going to be held more accountable—we with Bibles or those who have none? As our Father looks at our hearts and theirs, I wonder if tears run down His cheeks as they have mine today.

I am so thankful for that experience, even though I am not proud of the fact I didn't even think to ask if they had a way to do what I was going to teach. I look at the Church in America and myself and ask our Father to forgive us:

*You have given us so much, and what have we done with what You have given? When I stand before You, will I be ashamed as I look at those who had so little and yet loved so much more than I did when I had so much? Again Father, forgive us and wake the Church up to what is on Your heart! Amen.*

LIVING OUR FAITH

# Cross Country

I had a new experience this last fall: my youngest grandson went out for cross country for the first time. I had another grandson who had run this race, but I was working at the time and did not get to see or be involved then. I knew nothing about the rules, the training, or anything at all. The race was a mile long, and as he began he could not run the entire distance; he had to stop and walk sometimes.

Then as he continued training, he got to where he could finish by running the entire mile, but not in a competitive time. As he proceeded, however, his time got better and better. I saw him learn to pace himself and build his endurance.

I started the season watching him at the starting place or in the middle of the race. I realized this was not a sport in which I could see the entire race. So by the middle of the season, I chose to sit at the finish line. I could at least see the finish—and it was there I learned a lesson for myself.

The race was laid out and runners would follow the markings before the race started so they knew the course and what it would involve. I was watching all of this so I could learn, but what I learned at the finish line was something I would have never expected. I watched these kids come along a straight path to a great big sign that said "Finish Line." And surprisingly to me, the coaches were yelling, "Sprint!" Now, these kids were dripping with sweat and very tired as they came to the end of their race. "Sprint" was the last thing I would have yelled at them!

Then one meet, I saw myself and a scripture. Paul says in 1 Corinthians 9:24–27 that we all run a race but there is only one prize, so we must run to win the prize. We are to run to win, not just to finish. I looked at my own life like it was this cross country event. I have run up hills, crossed over streams, run on some level ground and over hills. And now at my age of seventy-seven, I saw myself turning onto the final stretch toward the finish line. I could see the big sign ahead of me and heard my Father saying, "Sprint, Shirley, sprint!"

Now I had some decisions to make. Was I going to finish this race and be satisfied, or would I sprint with the intention of winning the prize?

I confess that my recliner looks real good and the clicker to the TV is real handy. Even though my TV is turned to a Christian channel, is there something more I need to do on the final sprint?

I saw my grandson learn that as you come around that turn where you see that big sign that marks the finish line, even though you are exhausted, you can reach down inside and pull up the strength to sprint. So I am in training in my life to sprint now that I see the finish line of my life. I am looking back at all the hills, valleys, and streams I have learned to run across and am preparing myself, especially my mind, to reach down deep and pull up the strength and power of the Holy Spirit. Then I can run this last leg with all my heart—and with the determination not just to finish but to win the prize as well!

LIVING OUR FAITH

# Moses and Aaron

While I was at a Bible study this week, the question arose of where Aaron came from and how he fit in to Moses' life before they went before pharaoh. We determined that Aaron was the older brother of Moses and had not seen Moses for forty years while Moses was with his father-in-law, where he was a fugitive from the pharaoh. When we ran references, we found him in Exodus 4.

Moses had just had the experience of the burning bush and had a long conversation with God. God told him to go to the children of Israel and tell them God had seen what was being done to them in Egypt and that He would bring them up out that land to a land of milk and honey. Then he was to go before the pharaoh with the elders of Israel and tell him to let Moses' people go!

Next, however, the conversation turned to Moses telling God all the reasons he was not the one to do this.

Does this response sound familiar? In Exodus 4:13 he even told God to please send someone else.

Notice in verse 14 that the anger of the Lord was kindled against Moses. You see, God told Moses, "Look, your brother Aaron who can speak well is coming out to meet you." God had already made the plans and set them into motion for Aaron to help Moses. In verse 27 He told Aaron, "Go into the wilderness to meet Moses" (KJV). So Aaron went and met Moses on the mountain of God and greeted him with a kiss. The word 'met' implies the idea of a forceful, direct encounter. We would call it a "bear hug." Now Aaron became the mouthpiece of Moses as Moses heard God and told Aaron what God had said.

As usual, I saw myself and probably many members of the Body of Christ in this passage of scripture. Our Father asks (or tells) us to do something or go somewhere and we immediately tell Him all the reasons why He has chosen the wrong person. The excuses start (as if He doesn't know us) and what I see is this: how we must grieve Him! We are saying to Him, "You really don't know what You are doing or You never would have picked me."

All the while, of course, He had already had a plan for Moses and Aaron was on his way. I know He wants us to be humble, but is it humble to tell Him He is wrong? Could it be a false humility?

In prayer one day, the Holy Spirit stopped me as I prayed all the details about the situation. He revealed to me that He really did have the plan and I didn't need to tell Him how to do it. My part, according to James 4:7, was to submit the situation to Him and resist the enemy so that He could put that plan into action. James even specifies that the enemy will "flee" when this happens! So can we now check our hearts and see if we are doing and going where He said? But we must not forget that Jesus said one thing is needful and that is to sit at His feet and hear His words. Let's learn and put into practice His Word and Way!

# Positive Plus Negative

One day the Holy Spirit said to me, "Shirley, to have power you must have a negative and a positive." I didn't understand. I did not want negative things in my life. So I asked Him to please explain. Then He used a car battery to give me a physical picture of what He was trying to show me in my spirit. He said if you have a battery that is completely charged up and fasten the positive cable to it, it still will not start the car until you place the negative cable onto the battery.

I did not have any knowledge about batteries and electricity that would confirm this, so I asked my son-in-law, who did confirm the truth of what I had heard from the Spirit. So I asked Him for more revelation, and He has been adding more and more since then.

The battery represents the fully charged power of God, and I represent the positive cable. To see the power and glory of God brought forth, I must take every negative situation and join that "negative cable" to the full battery so the full current of God's power will flow through me and through the negative situation!

Furthermore, when I see an unsaved person, I take hold of him in prayer and love and join him to that fully charged battery so that the power will flow through me and through him. In this way the current will bring him into a complete circuit of God's power.

Importantly, a battery will not function with only a negative cable, so a person or situation not yet joined to God's power supply with the positive cable will not have any usable power.

Also, if I have the positive and negative backwards, the battery will explode and the power that God meant for good will bring destruction! For we have all been given a choice of where we join our cable, and if we get it backward and think life runs by our own power or works, everything of use for good will instead bring the opposite of what God intended.

An example is the experience of Adam and Eve. The positive was God's plan for them; the negative, one tree they must not eat. When they joined into the negative and activated it without hooking it into the positive, which would have been obedience to God's direction, what God meant for blessing became death for them.

One last lesson: I know my husband had to keep the posts of the battery clean of anything that would build up and prevent the power from reaching the cable connection. I must keep my connection with the battery clean always of anything that would block the flow of power into the negative around me.

So I am learning to take every negative thing and join it into the positive, and to keep myself joined to the full power of God through Christ, "for in him dwelleth all the fulness of the Godhead bodily" (Colossians 2:9 KJV).

# The Hamburger

Everyone needs a friend like Phyllis. I met her years ago, when another friend told me that Phyllis wanted to study the Bible, and would I go and share with her and some friends. I had never done this and was a little uncomfortable, but I said "yes."

At that time in my life while studying the Scriptures, I was seeing just how religious I was. So many things I had seen in myself were all about rules and my own opinions, not what the Word of God said. So I said I would come on one condition: I would share the Word, but all I would ultimately do was love those women. I promised not to try to change them but to let God have His way with them.

What a trip! In their own words, they told me they came from the world, not the Church, and I soon learned what that meant. I had been raised in the Church, so I had never experienced anything like this before, but I held true to my promise just to love them. I am not sure 'just' is the right word because when you have never heard some of the language and opinions that were coming forth, it becomes a real adventure—but it was great!

Now, just a few weeks into this study, Phyllis had an experience in which she truly saw that if she had been the only person alive, Jesus would have died for her. She gave herself to Him and became one of the hungriest people I have ever seen for the Word of God We became close friends and shared Him with each other every day.

This was great for maybe two years, and then things took a real turn. See, one thing I learned at this time was that people in "the world" can be very real, and Phyllis was definitely *real*. As I share what began to happen between us, know that I truly believe God put her in my life to expose the things that were hindering me from serving Him when I didn't even know they were there.

I wanted to lose some weight and eat healthy, so I asked Phyllis if she would help me and pray for me. First lesson learned! When you ask someone like Phyllis to pray for you and help you, she is going to do it. She thinks you mean it. I had not experienced this in my religious walk. We ask for prayer and then go about our business, without remembering to pray, but not Phyllis!

She had to go to Columbus, and my young daughter and I went with her. On the way home we stopped at McDonald's for lunch. When Phyllis and I were done, my daughter Jan still had a good bit left that she could not eat. I went to reach for her food, when Phyllis reached for it and threw it in the garbage. Now, I had a great big smile on my face as Phyllis did what I had asked her to do—to *help me*. But inside of me, I was so angry! I wanted that hamburger! She had no idea I was mad because I had become very good at smiling at someone while I hid other emotions inside.

Well, it was later at home that I had to admit to myself that I had learned how to get extra food. I would order more for Jan than I knew she could eat so that I would be able to eat two hamburgers while only ordering one for myself. But that wasn't the end, for the Holy Spirit began to show me how much I did this not only in my eating but also with Him. I asked Him for help, and then when He tried to give it to me by taking things out of my life to answer my prayers, I could not see His love. Twisted, isn't it?

You see, the main thing I learned from Phyllis was that she loved me and would have done anything to help me. She really believed I wanted help. When I finally told her the truth about that day, she was so surprised, and I believe hurt, that it really threw her off for a while and we had to work on getting me to be honest. There have been other times, too, when the same type of thing happened between her and I. She shared with me that she thought people who went to church would be very real and honest, so I guess I taught her, too.

So my prayer for everyone is that the Holy Spirit would bring a Phyllis into your life and that the Church of Jesus Christ would become so honest—with ourselves and Jesus—that He could really show us who we are in His eyes and the eyes of the world.

# "Trust Me and Open Your Eyes"

While vacationing in the mountains in Tennessee, we came upon an amusement park. Of course, the kids and my husband thought that this sounded like fun. My problem was, it was located on the very top of a mountain. Now, I love the mountains, but with my feet on the ground. The way up and down that mountain was a little train or a ski lift, and I had a tremendous fear of height.

I rode the little train up, and it was so scary that by the time we reached the top, I couldn't breathe. I was in such panic that I didn't enjoy anything about that day as my kids and Jim rode rides and enjoyed everything.

All I could think about was how I was going to get off that mountain. Would it be the little train or the ski lift? The thought of either one brought sheer panic.,

Well, my husband made the decision for me and with my eyes closed in total panic, he helped me onto the ski lift. Again I could not breathe and would not open my eyes. Very sweetly, my husband laid his hand on my arm and said, "Trust me and open your eyes." I did and I saw the most beautiful and wonderful sight! I looked and saw the majesty of my Father in those mountains. They were beyond beautiful, and I'm not sure 'majestic' describes the sight I saw.

That day changed by life. I realized what fear was robbing me of, and I determined to apply my husband's words to my life. You see, they were not just my husband's words but the words of Jesus to me:

"Trust Me and open your eyes!"

I began to apply these words in every area of my life—the good things, the bad things, all things that happened in my life. I opened my eyes to see Him and His love for me. It can be a mountain, it can be a valley, but if I trust Him and open my eyes, I will see and know Him.

For me, writing—including this book—is a way of sharing experiences in my life for which I am thankful. And I never would have had those experiences with my eyes closed!

LIVING OUR FAITH

# Running to Win

As we mentioned previously, Paul talks about running a race in 1 Corinthians 9:24; but more than just running in that race, he says to run to win it! Anyone who has played sports or as I have, has had children who did, know there is a prize for winning. They also know the cost of that win or taking home the "prize." So, what race was Paul talking about, how did he say to win it, and how do we apply what he said to our lives?

The first thing that must be established is, you must run to win, not just to be a part of the race (see "Cross Country"). Those are two entirely different things. If I am running just to be in the race, I will show up for that race, but the things that must be done to win will not have been done. I might finish the race, but the "prize" will not be mine. When you have the heart and mindset to be a winner, you will pay the price before the race in your training.

I went back further in the scripture to see what race Paul was talking about and how he prepared. I believe we see his goal was to give the gospel to everyone. So even though he himself was free, he became all things to all men to gain more. He ran this race with all his heart, and in so doing became what was needed—so that they would hear him and he would win them with the gospel of Jesus Christ.

In 1 Corinthians 9:23 he tells why: "And this I do for the gospel's sake, that I might be partaker thereof with you" (KJV). There would be great discipline in this because I know he never went under the law to preach to those who were. I know he never laid down the strength he had found in Christ to become weak and frail spiritually. But he brought himself under subjection, so that he might be a winner of souls—a preacher of the gospel—and he laid everything down to do it.

In this I see there must be more than one way to witness and share the gospel, but I believe there has to be one goal, and that is to win the soul of the person. And you must be willing to bring yourself to where you do this led by the Holy Spirit and not by your own opinion.

I saw a testimony of a girl who just became the gold medalist at the Olympics several years ago in archery. She also was the world champion. When the reporters asked her secret, this was her answer: "My father taught me that everyone would be training to hit the bullseye so I should train to hit the center of the bullseye."

Can we see the difference? Are we just not willing yet to be as Paul and have the heart to become what our Father needs us to be to all men? Just think, Paul is still preaching to us! When he was writing to Timothy, he concluded, "I have fought the good fight. I have completed the course. I have kept the faith and now there is the crown.

May we as the Church finally get it: there is more to being a winner than just showing up for the race!

# Who Says I Am Old?

I am coming close to my eightieth birthday and have been thinking lately about living long. I have seven grandchildren and eight great grandchildren. Does that make me old? Or is it the gray hair that makes me old? Or is it the fact that my easy chair is becoming very inviting? What is it that makes me old? Let's take a look at that question from the eyes of our Father.

Every day I speak a scripture from Psalm 71:

> *O Father, thou hast taught me from my youth: and hitherto have I declared thy wondrous works. Now also when I am old and greyheaded, O God, forsake me not; until I have shewed thy strength unto this generation, and thy power to every one that is to come.* — ***Psalm 71:17–18 (KJV)***

Lately as I speak this scripture and have been meditating upon it, I have started looking to my future. Do I really believe that I could show His strength and power to others? Do I have enough time left to fulfill what He called me to do many years ago?

Then I hear Paul say in Philippians 3:13–14:

> *Brethren, I count not myself to have apprehended, but this one thing I do: forgetting those things which are behind, and reaching forth unto those things which are before, I press toward the mark for the prize of the high calling of God in Christ Jesus.* **(KJV)**

This reminds me of running a race, when the finish line is getting closer and closer. I know when runners run a long race and they are nearing the finish line, every muscle aches and they think they just can't go on. At that point a decision has to be made in the mind, not just based on feelings. Could it be there are a lot of grandmas and grandpas that fit this picture?

I, for one, have decided I will finish this race and will be able to say with Paul in 2 Timothy 4:7, "I have fought a good fight, I have finished my course, I have kept the faith..." (KJV). Grandmas and grandpas, will you join me and others who have made this decision?

As I look at our nation and our schools, I ask, "Do we really have a choice?" You see, I remember when one woman took prayer out of our schools and we stood by and let it happen. Then came the decision to take the Ten Commandments out and we stood by again. I have repented for my part in this lack of faith that I could have done something to stop these things.

But today I see what one woman did and I ask myself, "What could a group of grandparents do who would join together and say, 'Enough is *enough*'?" We may have failed to do something at that time, but our race is not over yet.

As I look at the world's situation, I believe we are beginning to see the finish line. I believe the aches and pains of this last part of the race are catching up with us. But come on, grandparents, take a deep breath and determine to cross that line. After all, has it not been His strength that brought us this far? Has it not been His grace and mercy that brought us this far?

And so I pray that you all will begin to declare with me the scripture I started out with: "He will not forsake us until we have shown His strength and power to everyone." I love being a grandparent, and instead of murmuring and complaining about how things are, let's repent of our part in all of this and remember and put into practice: *The joy of the Lord is our strength* (Nehemiah 8:10)!

# *Notes & Reflections*

# Prayer and Worship

PRAYER AND WORSHIP

# Looking for an Intercessor

When I read Isaiah 59:16—"And he saw that there was no man, and wondered that there was no intercessor" (KJV)—my heart begins to cry out, "May I be one that You can find ready to be that intercessor!" I saw that it is a prophecy about Jesus, so I knew that I needed to study Him and how He did it. I saw in Hebrews 7:25 that He not only became that intercessor while He was on earth but He also lives to make intercession for us. So I set out to learn how to be an intercessor.

I tried and tried to pray and take it to whatever I thought intercession was. I read books and listened to teachers and tapes. I fasted and did everything I knew to do and some things where I didn't even know what I was doing. The one thing I had going for me was that I was determined to be what He needed and I sure wasn't going to give up, though many times I felt like it and I am sure He was waiting on me just to stop and listen to Him.

This journey began many years ago, and over the years, one step at a time, He has been so faithful to teach me and my friends. You see, in 1 Timothy 2:1, Paul is teaching Timothy that there are different forms of praying: there are "supplications, prayers, intercessions, and giving of thanks" (KJV).

What does all of this mean? I thought we just said our prayers and that was it! But not so, I learned. What I learned has become a desire of my heart for the Body of Christ. How He still needs not only pray-ers but also intercessors! I believe today He is still searching for those who will discern the differences between the different forms of prayer.

First, let's look at prayers. You can have a prayer list or someone's need on your heart. There are also prayer chains, in which our needs are passed on to others for prayer. These are all very important, but they are not intercession.

Second, let's look at intercession. Intercession is when the Holy Spirit speaks a need of the Father into your spirit and asks you to pray for His need, not yours. So basically, the difference between the two is that prayer is you bringing your need to the Father while intercession is God bringing His need to you. What a difference!

So the first thing I learned is that no one can teach you to intercede; they can teach you prayer, but not intercession. Learning to intercede comes from time spent with the Father, really learning to know Him, and from God coming to see that He can trust you with His needs and that you will not ever break His confidence but will be a trusted friend.

I will share just one of the experiences that means so much to me because what He asked me to intercede for greatly affected my grandson and our family. He was in Iraq, and we had no idea where he was as he could not share that information with us. One Sunday morning I got up with him so on my heart, I could not think of anything else. I prayed for him, and then I began to intercede as the Holy Spirit made it more and more real that He had a great need to intervene on behalf of my grandson. I shared the burden I had with his mom and dad and those who had gathered at my house that day. We continued to intercede for him until it seemed the burden lifted. I wrote down the timeframe when we prayed and looked forward to him coming home so I could see if something special had happened.

Guess what? When he came home, I asked him if there was something about that time, and he told me the most precious story a grandma could hear. At that very time we had prayed for him, he was leading a group of men into a village to clear it out for the rest of the soldiers that were coming. His orders were to go into the village and turn right down that street, check out buildings and houses and make sure it was safe. As he approached the village, he kept hearing "*Go left*" and he thought, "But my orders are to go right!" He said "go left" would not leave him, however, and it got so strong he told his men the orders were being changed to go left instead of right. Sure enough, there was a building to the left and when they searched it, they found a sniper.

But that is not the end of the story. As they now went to the right, a man dressed in the garb of that village ran out, right up to my grandson, and said to look into the garbage can that was up the street from them. My grandson said this just does not happen, that the locals would warn him. So he ordered the men who handled bombs and such to check it out. Sure enough, there were enough explosives in the garbage can to have killed all of his men and him if they hadn't caught the sniper first.

They took care of everything, and my grandson looked for the man who had warned him. He was nowhere to be seen. Now, you can believe anything you want, but this grandma believes an angel showed up to save him and his men because my Father saw a need that I could not see and asked me to intercede, not just lift His name up as a ritual.

As I write this, I am so thankful the Father did not give up on me as I tried to teach myself and learn from others how to intercede. And may I encourage the Body of Christ, myself included, to keep on drawing closer and closer to our Father and our High Priest, who ever lives to make intercession for us. May our heart be to hear the heart of the Father!

PRAYER AND WORSHIP

# Whose Shoes Will I Fill?

A few years ago I was asked to come to a women's meeting in St. Clairsville to speak. They told me they had been studying intercession and wanted me to teach on that subject and show them how to become an intercessor. I told them I would come, and then I set out to pray and study the Word so I could put together a great teaching.

After several days of this, I came to the conclusion that something was wrong. I could not put anything together. Finally, I realized I could not teach intercession. I could only teach the heart you must have to be an intercessor. Then my mind went back to the first time I experienced a major lesson in prayer from my Father.

My family had just moved to our farm, which was a huge event in the life of my oldest son. He was a freshman and was moving to a school that had always been a rival in the past. My husband and I thought we would do something to introduce him to his new schoolmates, and them to him. So, we planned a hayride and wiener roast for his whole class. We asked friends of ours to come and help. All the plans had shaped up, and work orders were given. My husband and the husband of my friend would take the kids on the hayride, our boys would gather and place the wood to roast the hot dogs, and guess what my friend's and my assignment was? Our job was to light the fire under the wood when the men left on the hay ride so the firewood would burn down and be just right for roasting. How hard could that be?

Everything was going according to schedule. Everyone was gone on the wagon, and my friend and I headed for this huge pile of wood with matches drawn. We lit it, but no one could have prepared us for what happened next.

Our children had constructed this pile of wood on the leaves that had fallen off the trees, as it was fall at the time. But the problem was, there were solid leaves covering the entire hill. Much to our fright, the fire took off and the whole hill was in danger of being ablaze. It was spreading so fast, it was one of those times when you know you should do something, but this was way beyond us. My friend and I looked at each other, and she said, "I think we need to get help!" She was thinking the fire department, but I fell to my knees. "Oh, well!" she thought, and fell to her knees, too.

Without a thought I prayed one of the sincerest prayers I have ever prayed: I cried, "Help, Father!" Then one of the most unexpected things happened. That fire reversed itself and burned right back down into that pile of wood! We looked at each other, and she said to me, "I think I meant the fire department." The wagon returned, and everything went on as planned.

As I thought about how you prepare your heart to intercede for others, I took a good look at this day and my simple prayer. Doesn't the answer to that prayer show us the Father's heart? I cried out from my heart and He answered.

Let's examine that prayer. One, it is founded on great fear. I know I did not have great faith to believe for this fire to burn back to the wood, for I could never have dreamed of anything like it. My friend and I are still amazed.

Two, there were only two words. But don't we have to pray longer than that and say just the right thing? Apparently not!

Three, my friend and I did not take the time to look at all the details of the situation and see if we knew all we should know. Nor did we ensure we were in agreement so we could pray for just the right thing so God would do it. I did not even pray, "Thy will be done," or say "amen" at the end!

I learned a simple lesson that day about our Father's response to our heart's cry: prayer, and especially intercession, is so much more that a set of perfect words, expressed just right. I have a concern for the Body of Christ where prayer is concerned. There are books written that give us ten steps to answers, or three steps to answers, and on and on. They tell us if you do this and that, you will see mighty things.

Now, I believe there is much to learn, but is there a formula? My grandma was a woman of prayer. Every afternoon she went into her bedroom, the door was closed, and she spent that time in prayer. We all knew not to bother her, for this was a big part of her life. So now here I come and have found a fulfillment in my prayer life—but do I have to do what Grandma did and set aside every afternoon? Is that the secret, or do I look to her life and her love for Jesus and her family, especially for a little granddaughter who loved her very much?

So today I want us to look at whose shoes we are trying to fill. Are they the shoes of some great teacher, author, pastor, or friend? Do we say, "I could never pray like them"? I suggest we look to Ephesians 6:15 and have our feet shod with "the gospel of peace," ready to face any situation with the knowledge of the love of God and bring that situation to Him, knowing He wants to answer it more than we want to pray it. May our life's goal be to walk in *His* shoes!

PRAYER AND WORSHIP

# A Knock at the Door

Many years ago, when I was just beginning to see the importance of prayer, a friend of mine and I read a book. This book was the story of two women who met each week and had prayer together. They told great stories of how God would bring people to their door right while they were in prayer, and they told of the ministry this had become. It sounded good to us, and we thought we would try it.

So we prayed the same prayer these women had prayed and looked forward with excitement to see what God would do. We were sure He would bring people to us also. We decided to meet each Wednesday morning and be really open to whatever happened. Fast forward to the next Wednesday: we met at my house and were so ready for anything! We had hardly bowed our heads when there was a knock at the door. We looked at each other and said, "Yes, we are ready to go!"

I went to the door and found a man standing there. As soon as I had opened the door, and I mean immediately, he screamed these words to me: "Satan himself is down in my car!" Oh, this is not what we expected. He turned and marched away, and my friend and I just looked at each other. Or maybe you could say we pleaded with each other without saying a word. *What on earth do we do now?* Those women in the book never mentioned an experience like this!

Well, we had prayed, and now we had to act. Very hesitantly, we walked outside and down the walk to the car. There sat a woman who screamed that the man needed to be committed for help. I tried to think of what to say, but I was shaking so hard I couldn't even think, let alone speak. Finally, I prayed one of my famous prayers: "Father, *help!*"

And help He did. We just kept quiet and waited for the man to come back to the car. He got in, and while the woman was still screaming, they headed out the driveway. You never saw a prayer meeting like the one that took place when my friend and I went back into the house! We cancelled all the prayers we had prayed, we pled for mercy, and we promised never again to follow what someone else had been led to do.

Looking back, this was such a good lesson. I would not trade it for anything—but I don't ever want to experience anything like it again. Later I found out that the man wanted to buy a car my husband had for sale, and the woman did not want him to spend the money.

May I share my heart with you? I love to read books, and I love to hear testimonies of what God has done in other people's lives, but there is a great danger if you start applying their experiences to your life, especially in areas where you have no prior experience or training.

I have such a desire in my heart for everyone in the Body of Christ to read His Book, seek Him, and find their own experiences. It would be so wonderful if each cell in His Body really came to know Him and then wrote a book about their journey. Let's start today!

# Here I Am, Lord—Send Me!

This week in studying when Saul (who became Paul) had his encounter with Jesus on the road to Damascus, I saw something I had never seen before. Acts 9 it tells the story of his experience, recounting that "suddenly there shined round about him a light from heaven: and he fell to the earth and heard a voice saying unto him, 'Saul, Saul, why persecutest thou Me?'" (Acts 9:3–4 KJV). Jesus then revealed who He was and gave Saul directions to "go into the city, and it shall be told thee what thou must do" (Acts 9:6 KJV). And they led him by the hand into Damascus, where "he was three days without sight" (Acts 9:8–9 KJV).

But the Lord appeared to a man named Ananias, who said, "Behold, I am here, Lord" (Acts 9:10 KJV). Then the Lord told him to go and find a man called Saul who was praying, and who had received a vision of Ananias coming and putting his hand on him to receive his sight (Acts 9:11–12).

Now, Ananias had heard of Saul and what he had been doing to the Church (Acts 9:13–14), and I am sure he had some thoughts that this did not sound right. But the Lord said, "Go!" and he went (Acts 9:15–17).

I have heard this story and read it many times, but I had never seen what I want to share with you now. Let's look at the importance of our prayers toward other members of the Body of Christ. Let's also look at the importance of obedience. But let's not forget humbling ourselves before the Lord. Now let's look at some what-ifs:

What if when the Lord encountered Saul, he had said, "Lord, why would You send me into the city to be shown what I must do?" What if he had said, "Lord, *You* could open my eyes right now if You would lay hands on them." Would he have had the vision of Ananias coming if he had refused to go to the city without knowing the details? Would he have ever regained his eyesight? Would he ever have fulfilled the purpose he was chosen for? I have been thinking about this a lot.

And then there was Ananias. What if he had said, "Oh no, this must be a trick to bring harm to me"? What if he had said, "I am not going into this dangerous situation, this cannot be the Lord!" What if he had not been in a place of fellowship with the Lord where he knew Him and knew it was the Lord who was speaking? The Lord stressed to Ananias that Saul was praying and had also had a vision.

So, what if Saul had not prayed? Could any of this story have taken place without prayer? I am seeking more and more revelation about the power of prayer, and not only prayer but also obedience to what I am shown in prayer.

Could some of the problems in our assemblies today be the result of the lack of prayer? I do not mean a quick, repetitive string of words, but the prayer that says, "Here I am Lord, send me." And I do not mean we have to travel miles to a faraway place. I mean, do I care enough about the Body of Christ to let the Lord send me to one of them for prayer, direction, and the power that comes from two in agreement? Am I willing to get instruction in prayer to go to my brother or sister to pray that their eyes get opened? Do I let fear or busyness cause me to say, "No Lord!"?

I guess where I am right now is facing the attitude that says, "I can do it myself and my way," and not seeing that we are a Body that needs every cell to be knit together in *love*. So I want to challenge all of us to take a good look at ourselves and recommit to being a true pray-er. And especially I challenge the grandmas to become a light to this generation in our praying and in our testimony of His goodness to us!

PRAYER AND WORSHIP

# Misunderstanding the Woman at the Well

All of us who have taught that the Samaritan woman Jesus addressed at the well was an adulteress (see John 4) will have to repent to her on the great judgment day. In all of Jesus' dialogue with this woman, He did not mention sin. Though He told her the history of her life, He did not intimate that she was living in sin. We deduced that she was because we did not understand the customs of the day.

A Jewish rabbi explained the fallacy of our interpretation of this passage of Scripture to me. The law of the day allowed a woman who was widowed to marry her deceased husband's brother. He was responsible to raise up seed for his brother. Apparently, the Samaritan woman had been widowed five times and was engaged to the sixth brother. The custom of the day did not allow a Jewish or Samaritan woman to speak to a man on the street. But after she had married five brothers, she was allowed to speak to men and men were allowed to speak to her.

It is a Jewish custom also that when a woman is betrothed to a man, she is brought to the groom's home before marriage, not to consummate the relationship, but to take on the family traits. For this reason Jesus said to her, "He whom thou now hast is not thy husband..." (John 4:18 KJV).

According to our Western mind, to "have" a man who is not your husband means you are involved in an adulterous relationship. Not so in the Jewish tradition. It simply refers to a time of betrothal.

My Jewish rabbi friend explained this custom to me and asked if I thought Ruth the Moabitess was an adulteress. I responded vehemently, "Of course not." Yet she did sleep at the feet of Boaz before they were married. That was what she was instructed to do by Naomi, and following her mother-in-law's suggestion in no way violated moral law.

The Samaritan woman called Jesus a prophet because He knew she had been married to five brothers, not because He had discovered her supposed life of sin. There was no mention of sin. The subject of their conversation was worship.

The greatest truth revealed through the encounter with the woman at the well is that God seeks people to worship Him "in spirit and in truth" (John 4:23 KJV). That requires revelation by the Holy Spirit to our spirits, taking us from religious questions regarding where we should worship, such as the Samaritan woman asked, to an encounter with the living God, which she unknowingly had. She realized that Jesus was a prophet, and when she had returned to her city, her zeal indicated that she had received revelation of God. She became an effective evangelist because of her encounter with Jesus.

PRAYER AND WORSHIP

# A Spark

I awoke this morning with a line from the song "Pass It On" by Kurt Kaiser running through my mind: "It only takes a spark to start a fire burning." Then I thought of a ladies luncheon I attended yesterday. It was a special meeting, and let me explain why.

The Scriptures say we should "assemble" (see Acts 4:31, Acts 11:26), not just gather together—and this was truly an assembly. There was no speaker, but every person there brought that spark of who they are, what Jesus has done for them, and what He means to them. There was fun and laughter. There was a testimony of healing, a testimony of the leading of the Holy Spirit, a testimony of the turnaround of a son who had been changed from a wrong lifestyle to a right one. There was a celebration of the life of a friend who had passed into the very presence of the Lord. There was even a mouse who testified of his relationship with Jesus! There was fellowship at lunch with great food prepared by many.

Though most meetings open with praise and worship, this one closed with it as several women shared their giftings and talents of music. The presence of the Holy Spirit was so real! As I left that meeting, and still today, I am warmed on the inside by the sparks that lit a fire in me.

My prayer is that each woman there would carry their spark with them, and that it would flow and light other sparks until we see the fire of His glory over this entire region. But I pray this not only about those at this meeting, but also about all the sparks who claim Jesus. How this would bless our Father as we join our sparks together and accept the sparks that are in each one of us! On second thought, it would not only bless Him, but oh—how we would also be blessed as the Holy Spirit blows on those sparks and they become a flaming fire!

PRAYER AND WORSHIP

# Watch for the Kick

While teaching a Bible study last week, I shared something that had happened to me years ago in my adventure to becoming a farmer's wife. I am tempted to think that the problem was my husband, who was just becoming a farmer, but honestly, both of us knew just enough to be dangerous.

One of the first things we wanted to do was buy a cow and have our own milk and whatever else a cow produced (like butter, cheese, cottage cheese, and anything else that was called "dairy"). So we went cow shopping. We found a young Jersey cow, and we were told that they produce a very rich milk. That sounded good to us, so Jennie, as we would call her, came to our farm.

My husband worked some afternoons, and this day was one of those times, so my father-in-law came down to show me how to milk a cow. Looking back, I think I believed I would learn how to milk the cow before I went shopping.

We went to the barn and he began to teach me. Oh boy, what a scene! The cow would not let him near and began to kick so hard and often that he had footprints down the front of him. He looked at me and said, "This cow has got to be milked, and you are going to have to try." Yeah, right!

But a good farmer's wife does what she has to do, so I took a deep breath and approached Jennie very carefully. I started saying, "Nice cow," apparently thinking that was the surefire way to tame an unruly beast.

To my amazement, however, she never moved at all. I sat down beside her and started doing what my father-in-law said to do. Guess what? I ended up with milk in the bucket. I was so tickled with myself.

But then came the morning, and she would not let my husband near her, either. What was wrong with this picture? Again I went in and she never moved, letting me milk her again and again—always.

An old farmer came to visit us and asked how we were doing with the new cow. Of course, I shared my ordeal of having to do all the milking, both morning and night, and I asked him if he had any answers for me—and he did. He asked me who raised the cow, and I told him we got it from an older lady who lived alone. He began to laugh and said that was the key. Jennie was raised by a woman and only knew how to be in the presence of a woman. I later shared with my husband that I didn't care what breed of cow he bought anymore, I just wanted to know who raised her.

So after sharing this story at Bible study recently, I drove down the road wondering why exactly I had shared it. The next morning I woke up wondering the same thing—but then I saw the reason. What the Holy Spirit was wanting to show me now, years later, was that we all are the end product of who raised us and how they did it.

I then saw the Body of Christ. We all come from different doctrines, and we do "kick" when someone from another belief system comes near. When we hold such valuable giftings inside of us—not unlike the cow's milk and all the products that come from it—exposure to others in the Body of Christ pulls those giftings out of us to be used by our Father for His purposes. How dangerous it is, then, to start kicking!

I am so thankful for what I have learned from worshipping with Native American believers, with my Kenyan brothers and sisters, and in many different ways of worship in my area and even other parts of the country. I have learned to pretend I have a bookshelf I cannot see, but in my mind it is very real. On that bookshelf I place everything I do not understand, and my Father takes it down and reveals to me if it is of Him or if I should let it go.

I have learned to dance and worship with bongo drums, flutes and drums, and even guitars, drums, and whatever else our young people use. I worship on Sunday mornings with liturgies and music that seem different to many. I also have learned there doesn't have to be musical instruments. I can come into worship without adding a sound to His presence.

So as I look back at the Jersey cow experience, I think the important thing is the *presence*. She knew a woman's presence, and I believe the Body of Christ must have fellowshipped with the Holy Spirit in their own life to the degree that they recognize Him wherever they find Him. Isn't it true? If we kick every time something we don't understand comes into our life, we could be falling into the very thing we were warned about in Scripture: "And the eye cannot say unto the hand, I have no need of thee: nor again the head to the feet, I have no need of thee" (1 Corinthians 12:21 KJV). Then how in the world will we ever release and receive the fruit that is in each other?

Therefore, watch for the "kick"—it could be keeping us from the truth as we react quickly instead of knowing His presence wherever we find it.

# *Notes & Reflections*

# Holy Days and Holidays

HOLY DAYS AND HOLIDAYS

# Call a Solemn Assembly

During a Bible study I was participating in, Joel 2:15 was brought up for us to look at. It says, "Blow the trumpet in Zion, sanctify a fast, call a solemn assembly..." (KJV). Now, of all the words in this scripture, "call a solemn assembly" stood out. I had no idea what that meant, and it sounded like it would be something very somber and serious. I love to study what the Jews did under the old covenant because I believe it is a picture of what Jesus fulfilled. I do not want to go back under the law, but I'd love to have what I should reap from it because of what Jesus did. So I began a study on the internet of the meaning of 'a solemn assembly.'

What I found out has become part of my life and preparation for the celebrations of my church life. A solemn assembly consists of eight days. For seven days they prepared themselves for the eighth day. During these seven days they prayed, fasted, and dedicated themselves to the celebrating of the eight day. This was not a sad, somber thing but preparation for a day of celebration on the eight day.

Now, how do I apply this to my life through the finished work of Jesus? I looked at the special days we have in our denomination, and I began to call a solemn assembly in my life at these times. This included communion, passion week, John Hus Sunday, lovefeast, and any other day I needed to prepare to celebrate Jesus. So the week before communion, I would spend the prior seven days in consecrating myself to Jesus and what He did. I have a list of things that came with that Bible study, but you can make your own list of spiritual challenges that you are dealing with. This is the sample from that online study:

- Day 1: The call for consecration (beginning in Joel 1–2)
- Day 2: Return to your first love.
- Day 3: Remove the idols in your heart.
- Day 4: Humble yourself and put away pride.
- Day 5: Be holy as God is holy.
- Day 6: Consecrate your home.
- Day 7: Restore broken relationships.
- Day 8: Renew your covenant with God and *celebrate* Jesus and what He has done for us.

By the way, the meaning for 'consecrate' in the dictionary is "to dedicate to the service of God." I am sure there is much more to learn, but even this basic understanding has made my walk with Him more meaningful and precious. May it be the same for you!

HOLY DAYS AND HOLIDAYS

# God Is Love

What a great month February is! Hearts, roses, and boxes of candy are everywhere. It surely is a time to tell your sweetheart that you love them.

But something else is on my heart this year. It is a simple question, but takes a lot of nerve to answer it. John tells us that if we say we love God and hate our brother we are a liar—"for he that loveth not his brother whom he hath seen, how can he love God whom he hath not seen? And this commandment have we from Him, That he who loveth God love his brother also" (1 John 4:20–21 KJV).

So here comes the simple question that is not hard to answer: Do I love God? Do I love Him with all my heart, all my strength, and all my mind? Or as many people will do this Valentine's Day, will I run to the store at the last minute and hope they have some roses or candy left so I can hand it to the one I say I love, thereby fulfilling my duty of not forgetting them on this special day?

Is it possible I do this with my Father? I say I love
Him. I even go to church every Sunday, I sing in the
choir and do anything else they ask me to do. But is it
possible I do it all with people I have bad feelings
toward, or that I go out another door so I do not have to
run into them? Do I love them with all my heart? Or is
Sunday like a Valentine's Day, where one day a year, or
one day a month, or maybe even one day a week, I hurry
to do something that I believe will tell God, "Of course I
love You"?

After the Holy Spirit asked me this question—all of
those questions!—everywhere I went in the Scriptures I
found something about love. But then it hit me, of course
this would be true—because *God is love*. So it follows in
1 John 2:4, "He that saith, I know him, and keepeth not
his commandments [to love his neighbor], is a liar, and
the truth is not in him" (KJV)

There were some people who were easy to love, and
then there were those about whom I said, "Father, if You
don't give me love for this one, I'm done." But then His
mercy and goodness show up. For if I am willing to do
it, He is more than willing to give me the love I need to
be obedient. What a good Father we serve!

About the same time, I came across a song that the
Gaithers wrote, entitled "I Will Serve You Because I
Love You." You see, I have found that my motives are
so important to my Father. Why do I serve Him? Why do
I meet with those who claim to love Him? Is it to look
right—like a quickly purchased box of candy—or is it
because I am so touched by His love for me that
everything I do, including loving others, is because *I love*

*Him*? As we come into the Lenten season, may we look long and hard at the simple question: Do I *love* God?

HOLY DAYS AND HOLIDAYS

# Play It As It's Written

Several years ago, because I love to play the piano, I decided to buy a keyboard. My thinking was that I could push a few buttons and be accompanied by all kinds of instruments, including the rhythm section. Well, what a surprise I was in for!

I like to play a song the way I feel it. Sometimes I like to hold a note because I am really into the words and I just need to "feel the moment." Guess what? That rhythm section on my keyboard plays with no feeling. Every beat is right on time and very definitely not programmed to my heart.

So I went to a friend who is advanced in playing the piano yet plays so much from her heart. You don't even have to know music to know this is true, for her music also touches your heart. I asked what I had found to be a tough question: "How do you play your music from your heart? I can't make it work on my keyboard!" Her answer was so simple it stunned me. She said, "You play it the way it is written from your heart."

A light bulb went off in my head. I thought, "Duh!" To this day she cannot remember our conversation, but it has brought understanding to my life in many areas.

I was in the band, orchestra, and choir in high school, and I have always sung in the church choir, so I have performed in many situations where this concept of hers was valid. If you are going to play or sing in one of these types of groups, you have to play the music the way it is written. The key must be right, the timing must be right, you must take a rest if that is written on your part, and you must play the notes you are given. Can you guess where I am going?

Our Father only asks for a joyful noise when we are singing to Him alone. So when alone, I can play and sing any way I feel it. But if I am going to be a part of bringing harmony to the Body of Christ, I am going to have to play my part the way it is written. What if an orchestra came together and decided to play the song the way they each felt it? What if they each decided they wanted to play a different song that day? What would that sound like? What our Father intended to produce a beautiful sound of harmony to the listener would be nothing but chaos and noise.

As my friend and I talked about this one day, we thought about team sports. Any team game requires discipline not to come out on the court or field and do your own thing. There is no more doing or playing according to however I happen to feel that day. The coach has a plan, and it only works if I play it like it is written with all my heart. With music, the conductor chooses the music and hands out their part to each section of different instruments, and the only way you will continue to be a part of that production is if you play your own part as it is written.

I had an opportunity to sit in on our organist and pianist practicing duets for the Christmas services at my church. They are both so talented in their own right, but I watched and listened to them stop and go over and over different parts they were having trouble playing in time with each other. What an example to me of playing it the way it is written with all your heart! They made sure it would bring forth the message and sound the composer wrote from his heart. I had never thought of the composer's heart when I sang or played a part until my pianist friend shared with me the importance of playing the music the way the composer wrote it.

So this Valentine's Day, which is all about the heart, may we take this thought to the Body of Christ and our Father's heart: He has written a beautiful song that He wants and needs His people to play. It has many different parts, but if every person plays their part the way it is written with all their heart, the message of Jesus and what He did for us will be heard in many different ways. We have many forms of music in the world, and so does our Father. When we let Him train us on our own instrument (or gifting) and then be so happy just to play our own part, instead of trying to tell our brother or sister how to play theirs, what a sound that must be to Him!

I believe when Jesus prayed we would be become one (John 17:21), that is exactly what He meant. Isn't it exciting to think that our Father can take all of us, each so different, and if we will play it the way *He* wrote it with all our heart, it will minister to Him as well as to a world that badly needs to know they are loved? The world needs to know that we need them to come and join us with their gifting so the song continues to become more and more like what He wrote.

# Sand or Rock?

Don't you appreciate how Jesus used parables to teach? They make us think, and we have to take them back to Him to understand them. I believe when we ask Him to explain what He meant and not rely on our own interpretations, the Holy Spirit is quick to respond.

At this time of the year, as I have been preparing to celebrate His death, burial, and resurrection, the parable of the houses built on the sand and the rock is in my thinking. As I studied it, I saw that a storm hit both houses, so that was not the difference. One was built on sand, and one was built on rock. So the difference was the foundation the houses were built on. I have studied long enough to know He was not stopping there, however. There had to be more!

I read it over and over. What are the sand and the rock in the parable? And then I saw it—it was there the whole time:

*Therefore, whosoever heareth these sayings of mine and doeth them, I will liken him unto a wise man, which built his house upon a rock. ... And every one that heareth these sayings of mine, and doeth them not, shall be likened unto a foolish man, which built his house upon the sand.* — **Matthew 7:24–29 (KJV)**

You see, I have found in my own life that I can think I know something, and maybe really do in my head, but getting it into my heart where it becomes a part of me and I actually become a *doer* of the words of Jesus is something entirely different.

So as we prepare to celebrate His resurrection, by which He gives us the power to become a *doer*, may we make a deeper covenant with Him to dig deep, very deep, until we have gone so deep that we hit rock and then start to build off of that foundation.

Of course, here comes more truth in that parable: *He* is that rock! Obedience is the key to building on it. I pray we dig and dig until we have removed every religious tradition, every misconception, and everything that would hinder us from being obedient and reaching the place where our whole being is founded on the Rock of obedience.

# "Will You Also Go Away?"

With the celebration of the resurrection of Jesus happening this month, my heart is drawn back to different times of my life when this was a meaningful season for me. And there is great excitement on Sunday morning as we celebrate His victory over death and the fact that He is alive! Now we can sing with the Gaithers, "Because He lives I can face tomorrow, because He lives all fear is gone!" (see "Because He Lives!"). But is it?

My favorite service is communion on Thursday night, when we remember Jesus' experience in the Garden of Gethsemane. I am thinking of the times Jesus needed the disciples and they were gone. Over the years the Holy Spirit has shown me the many times He needed me and I was gone, so let's look at some relevant scriptures and change anything that needs changed to ensure we will be there with Him.

John 6:66 tells us that "many of his [Jesus'] disciples went back, and walked no more with him" (KJV). Jesus then turned and asked the Twelve, "Will ye also go away?" (John 6:67 KJV). He had been telling them that they must eat of Him, that it was by the Spirit and His Word that they would have life. I think their answer is interesting: they said, "Lord, to whom shall we go?" (John 6:68 KJV). It could sound like they considered going away.

Then, in Matthew 26:36–46, His disciples abandoned Him again. As He was preparing Himself for what was ahead, He asked Peter, James, and John to come a little farther than the others, to pray with Him. As He fell on His face and was "exceedingly sorrowful," they fell asleep. His question to them was, "What, could ye not watch with me one hour?" (Matthew 26:40 KJV). The sad part was that He knew they needed that time of prayer so they would not enter into temptation. Do you suppose that if they had prayed, they would not have denied Him?

Luke 19:41 says He beheld Jerusalem "and wept over it" (KJV). Matthew 23:37 says He longed to have gathered His people together as a hen gathers her chicks under her wings, but they would not cooperate. I also think of the times He shared and shared with them and they did not get it. How He longed to fellowship with them in truth! I wonder how His Spirit was grieved.

Now, I want to share some of the reasons this season is so meaningful to me. You see, I have been guilty of all of the above. Fifty-three years ago this year, I was sitting in a Wednesday evening Lenten service watching a movie of the last week of His life. He was carrying the cross with blood streaming down His face from a mean crown of thorns. He looked into the camera (in the film) and said, "This I have done for you, what have you done for Me?"

In an instant I knew nothing I had ever done was for Him. Oh, I had taught Sunday school, directed the junior choir, attended all church services, and even read my devotions, but suddenly I saw my heart. It had all been because I was taught that was what I should do, or because I enjoyed it, or for other selfish reasons. I also realized at that instant, He had done everything because He *loved* me. No one took His life—He gave it after a tremendous struggle in the garden. So I went home and had my own garden experience. Would I lay down all my selfish reasons for doing anything and pick up His cross of walking in *love* and follow Him?

Then there are the many times I knew I should pray, and even tried, but guess what? I too fell asleep and missed the precious time of fellowship with Him. I guess I began to see He wants and needs me to spend time with Him. He needs me to be so in love with Him that I can't wait to see what He has to share with me today.

Then there was the day I was worshipping (I thought) while singing and playing my piano. I was singing songs like "He's All I Need" when in my heart I realized I was singing *about* Him, not *to* Him. I thought about how I would feel if I had prepared a great feast for my family and they all came and talked about me instead of to me. He has prepared so much for us, and we gather together and sing and talk about Him but not to Him. So, now my song has become, "*You're* all I need!"

When I think about taking up His cross and walking in love, I look at that cross while He was still on it. If He is my example and He says to love as He has loved, I have so far to go. I can tell you right now I have not come to the place where I would hang naked in the town square for my best friend, let alone my enemies. He did it and had to look down at His mother. He also looked down and only saw one disciple, John. I know He dealt with the pain of all of this when He was alone in the garden, but then He experienced it in the flesh as well. It was real pain!

So as this season comes and goes and we celebrate His resurrection, I don't ever want to forget the hurt in His heart as one by one His disciples left. Or even if they stayed, they were not seeing how much He needed them to understand His love for them and the world. My prayer is: *Jesus, reveal more and more to me that love and empower me to give it out to my family, the Body of Christ, the world, but most of all back to You first! I want to talk about You, but more than that I want to talk with You!*

## HOLY DAYS AND HOLIDAYS

# "Come, See a Man"

In sharing and studying with others about bringing people to Jesus, my mind has begun to think about who this Jesus is. Do I even know Him well enough to introduce Him to them as my friend?

Do I understand what He has done for me? Do I know what He would do in any situation that comes in my life? Do I know how to study His words and apply them so they bring truth in my life? Have I ever experienced His love? Have I ever experienced His love when I have done something that has hurt and displeased Him? Have I really seen that He has made a way for me to enter into the presence of our Father and come to a place of knowing Him also? Have I allowed and come to understand what it means that Jesus baptizes us with the Holy Spirit so I have Him as my Teacher, my Guide, the Giver of the power to walk out and experience the things Jesus died to give me?

So again my heart and mind goes to the Scriptures. I began to think of the woman at the well (this is what we call her) and how and what Jesus felt about her. There is so much in this story, but I am meditating on her from the Scriptures, not how we might have been taught about her (see "Misunderstanding the Woman at the Well"). Look at her response to Him telling her He had water such that if she would drink, she would never thirst again. Her immediate response was, "Sir, give me this water" (John 4:15 KJV). Then Jesus told her about herself and she perceived He was a prophet.

Here is where I see her heart: she had to have a hunger for something of God because her next question was about where to worship as a Samaritan. This freed Him to go on and tell her how the true worshippers will worship—with our spirit and in truth, rather than in a particular place (John 4:24). He even stated that is how we *must* worship.

Next she revealed to Him that she was expecting the Messiah called the Christ ("the anointed one"). Does this really look like the heart of an adulteress, as she is so often portrayed? When He heard her heart, He revealed Himself to her as that Messiah, the one who had come to tell her all things. The only other time that I know of when Jesus, in His walk before the crucifixion, revealed Himself as the Christ was when He asked Peter who he said He was and the revelation of who Jesus is was given to him.

Then came the disciples asking what He was doing talking to this woman. As I read this, my heart cries out for myself and the entire Body of Christ! Does the disciples' question sound familiar among today's believers? I am sure you know what I am saying. She leaves to tell the men of her city to "Come see a man, which told me all things that ever I did: is not this the Christ?" (John 4:29 KJV).

Look now at the teaching He gave His disciples (John 4:31–38). He took them to His Father's heart, saying, "Life up your eyes, and look to the fields; for they are white already to harvest" (John 4:35 KJV). Some men sow while others reaps, but we all enter into God's harvest.

Thus, some of the Samaritan men believed on the woman's words and then came to Him to hear His own words. They asked Him to stay and teach them. I love and am so blessed by these men's words: "Now we believe, not because of thy saying: for we have heard him ourselves, and know that this is indeed the Christ, the Saviour of the world" (John 4:42 KJV).

HAs we come into the Thanksgiving and Christmas seasons, I sense the heart of my Father saying to us that the harvest is white. Go tell! But my question is: Go tell what? Again, have I sat at His feet long enough to have the same conversation she had? Have I let Him show me myself as He sees me? Have I answered truthfully and repented and told Him I want to *know* Him? Have I allowed Him to become so close to me that I have been given by Him the revelation "You are the Christ"?

And then the burden that is really on my heart: Where do I then take these people I have told to "*Come* see a man"? Are the places where we say we go to worship prepared? Is it a true revelation of Jesus I am taking them to, or is it man's own thinking of who He is? Are they prepared to love and have compassion on those whom others would call unworthy? Has it become a religious gathering, or is it truly an assembly of forgiven people who have assembled to allow the Holy Spirit to lead as we worship in the Spirit and in truth?

It is not my place to judge, but my heart cries out for us to examine ourselves and our places of worship. Hear the heart of our Father saying, "My Son through the Holy Spirit is still sitting by the well (or wherever there is a hungry soul) waiting for someone who has experienced the revelation of who Jesus is to say, "*Come*, see a *man!*"

# Love Is the Mortar

As we approach Thanksgiving Day, I have been thinking of how thankful I am for my home, its furnishings, and every need met. You see, in praying for myself, my family, and my church assembly that I attend, I had a special thought that has given me much to consider. It became very real to me: a house is just a building until a family moves in and makes it a home, and what we call a church is just a building until His family moves in and makes it a home or dwelling place for Him.

So how does this all happen? I believe *love* has to be the foundation of any home. How can we build up anything of value if love is not at the very core of the plan? One day the Holy Spirit revealed to me that most of His children see the time they come together on Sunday morning or midweek study as a gathering. But if we study Scripture, we see He said to *assemble* ourselves, especially in the last days. So what is the difference?

Jesus said we are living stones in this Church He is building (1 Peter 2:5). So if we just gather together, we look like a pile of stones. We have no structure or no purpose. But if we assemble, we come to the services as stones in whatever size or shape we have been designed to function as. Then we say, "Jesus, assemble us as You see fit for what You want to build here!" Now we are no longer a pile of stones, but maybe something like a fireplace, where each stone is in its place and has a purpose. A fire could be built in it to keep others warm, and it also gives light to the space around it. It could be a place the family gathers around for food and fellowship and enjoying each other. I am sure He has a great plan for all assemblies!

When I was in Africa, I saw churches that were old chicken coops, and corrugated metal ones with manure floors. They had no Bibles, not even the pastors, but they knew Jesus and they definitely were assemblies. I have never experienced such worship or truer family assembled together by Jesus to worship Him! The prayer and intercession were beyond what I could ever put into words.

So I am thankful for what I have in my home and in my home church, but I truly desire that more and more, we become an assembly Jesus Himself has assembled together for a great purpose, and that those assemblies would spread out into our families, the area we live in, our nation, and then to the whole world. This takes us back to the beginning, for I believe *love* is not only the foundation but also the mortar that holds all those stones in place—the same way Jesus put them all together!

HOLY DAYS AND HOLIDAYS

# What Does Christmas Mean to Me?

I have always loved Christmas. The traditions I experienced as a child in my family were beautiful. We only exchanged one gift, but that was done in a wonderful way. Sometimes that gift was homemade but given with much thought and love. My grandpa was not very vocal during the year, but from Thanksgiving to Christmas Eve, it was his season to shine. We lived with my grandparents, and these memories have greatly influenced my life today.

My life was also influenced by the Christmas traditions of my church and my family there. The church I attend has wonderful services that celebrate Jesus' birth. The music, candlelight services, liturgies, food, and fellowship are tremendous! These all lead us to the new year, and to a recommitment to let our light shine and to lift Jesus and His ministry above everything else in our lives. Even as a child, when I lifted my candle high with the congregation in that dark sanctuary to show that one little candle lifted with many other little candles could light a room, my heart would cry out to do that somehow in the world.

Then one day I found myself in a remote village in Kenya, Africa. When I say remote, I mean remote. They had so little. It's still difficult to put into words what I saw. But one experience will never leave me.

I was helping another person with a children's outreach meeting. In fact, I was making peanut butter and jelly sandwiches for them. She had brought a few toys for them to play with after her teaching, one of which was a little football. She gave this football to a young boy of about twelve or thirteen. I looked up and saw the look in his eyes, and I saw he didn't know what to do with it. He had no idea what it was.

My thoughts went back to my boys, who had both played football, and I thought, "Come on Mom, you know enough to play some football with these boys!" So I left the sandwiches and went out to this boy. We spoke different languages, but I motioned to him to give me the ball. I threw it up into the air and caught it, then motioned to him that I was going to throw it to him. He looked puzzled but reached for it, and wow—we had completed a pass! Now I motioned for him to back up, and we got pretty good at those passes. As he began to relax, I saw such joy in his eyes and heard such laughter coming from him that I forgot how old I was and just enjoyed this time.

Then came the tears as I realized that here were children who had never even seen a ball, while my children had had one since they were born. My husband had bought a ball for the new babies while they were only days old.

That was only the beginning of my tears, for when I got home, one of the first things I saw was my dog playing with his ball. I know we have just celebrated Thanksgiving, and my prayer is that we really remain thankful, not just for big things but also for all of the little things that we take for granted. I never would have thought a little ball could so change my life. Christmas has never been the same since that day! If only I could somehow get the message to our children, even those who do not have a lot, that Christmas is not about more and more toys or whatever it is that they want these days. Rather, Christmas is about the birth and coming of a baby who would grow up and spend His entire life giving everything He was to a people who didn't deserve Him. What He asked of me was to love Him, to serve Him, to trust Him, to obey Him, to know Him, and to learn how to do this by doing all of these things to others.

I guess what put it all into perspective was that even my dog had a ball, in fact several balls, while in Africa there was a child who had never even seen one. I don't believe Jesus is angry that my dog had several balls, but I believe He is very grieved that on the day we celebrate His birth, our thoughts are on what we get not what we can give to others.

*Father, I pray this year especially for the people who claim to be followers of Jesus in our area to let our little lights shine so that those who have no hope or joy may see the light that all the little lights make and be drawn to Him. Then let us truly celebrate His birth and all it means to us!*

# Do I Have a Recipe?

While making Christmas cookies and candies with my daughter and her family, the memories of favorite recipes came up. Her husband remembered his grandma's favorite cookies, and when my daughter tried to make them for him, she could not find any recipe. Grandma had just mixed ingredients together without measuring and had never written down how she made them so the recipe, or knowledge of how to make them, was gone.

That reminded me of my mom's potato salad. She made the best that I had ever tasted. One day I asked her for the recipe, and of course there was none. She just mixed up what she knew went in, but that did not help me or my daughter, who wanted to have the recipe, too. So I asked her to please measure everything and write it down. She did this, and then I had the way to make the same wonderful potato salad.

Oh, but when I tried it something was wrong. It did not taste like hers. I asked her if she had forgotten one of the ingredients, or if I had forgetten something. She asked me how long I let the dressing set before I added it to the potatoes. There was nothing in the recipe that said to let it set before mixing, so no, I had not. Then she shared that this was such a part of her making the recipe she did not even think to write it down. Now when we make potato salad, it tastes like my mom's.

What on earth does this all have to do with the Bible? Well, I thought back over my life and realized I had been given a "recipe" many years ago for studying the Bible. You see, it is one thing to read the Scriptures and another thing to study them. I could read the words, but how do you study them? Then I read a book that gave me the recipe for study! It said the following:

- Pick a book of the Bible (I chose Ephesians).
- Begin reading until a verse or statement interests or speaks to you.
- In a new notebook, write the verse at the top of the page.
- Next, write down what you think it is saying.
- Then meditate and pray about how you can apply it to your life. Write out all this meditation and the prayer you are praying under the scripture. Be honest and open your heart to hear the answer to your prayer. Do this every day.

The Holy Spirit will teach you all you need to know about this recipe and will show you the little things you are doing or have done to change the recipe.

As I was praying today, I shared with a friend, and we had our own Bible study on the phone about what makes a recipe fail or why it needs to be written down. There were times I was busy and decided to cut out some of the directions in a recipe or change the ingredients, whether to save money or to save time. I shared with her how my husband could tell every time I used a different brand of tomato juice in my chili recipe. She shared with me that just a few days ago she had made her favorite meatloaf recipe and instead of taking the time to chop fresh onions, she used the dried onions in a jar. She said it changed the taste so much that dried onions probably would not be a choice in the future.

Have you ever added something at the wrong time and ruined what you were making? Is it possible I do this same thing with the recipe God has designed for my life?

I think I am seeing the importance of writing down the things I have learned that make my life better. When I get in a situation in my life where I forget what I knew in the past, I pull down one of those notebooks and read the recipe for what I learned in the Scriptures that got me through before.

What if Paul and the other disciples had not written the letters to the churches almost two thousand years ago? Where would we be? Would we be trying to live this Christian life by throwing a bit of this and a bit of that into our lives and the lives of others?

Over the years I have tried to pass my recipes on to my children and grandchildren. Maybe they will never make them, but if they ever have a memory surface in a Christmas or birthday celebration, they will have it written down, and they will be able to make it just like we did back in the past.

As to my writings as I have studied the Scriptures over the years: Will my children and grandchildren be able to open one of my notebooks and see my recipes for making my life so full? Will these writings remind them of something we did or shared in their childhood? Will they see the goodness and faithfulness of God in my writings? Will they see Jesus becoming more and more real in my life? I pray this is true!

So today I have gone from trying to make a cookie for which we did not have a recipe to seeing how important it is for me to write things down as I learn. I am so thankful for the times I took the time to ask my grandma how she made different recipes and for the times I went on walks as a young girl with her and learned to know her. She faced many hard times, but I never heard her complain. My favorite memory of her is when, every afternoon, she went into her bedroom, shut the door, and spent the afternoon in prayer. She had the recipe to life, and today I have looked back and committed myself to following that recipe of a life of prayer every day of this new year.

This year may we all check what recipe we are using. Is it going to give us the desired results? Are we really following His directions? Are we taking shortcuts? Are we changing what He says to something that seems easier? And let's make sure we are writing our recipes down for future reference—for ourselves and others to see and learn from.

HOLY DAYS AND HOLIDAYS

# 365 Days

Here it is again! Can you believe it? December 25, a day to celebrate our Savior's birth. But is it really?

My husband had a saying he told me and our children all the time: "It is not what you do on one day, it is what you do on the other 364 days."

We have always tried to celebrate the "special" days, like birthdays, Father's Day, Mother's Day, Christmas, and so on, but this year I am really remembering what he said. So I will celebrate Jesus this Christmas—but what have I done this year for Him, to Him, and by Him the other 364 days?

Have I come to know Him better? Have I seen Him in my brothers and sisters when I say I go to learn and fellowship with them where I worship? Or has worship of Him become a habit, something I am supposed to do?

Have I made my life a 365-day gift to Him, to be used as He wants, or do I give Him that gift on Christmas and then take it back to do what I want to do with it the other 364 days?

I have lived long enough to know He isn't looking for me to give many gifts to Him on Christmas so it looks like a great outpouring of my love for Him. *No!* He is looking and hoping for one gift. He is not looking for all of my sacrifices of prayer, study, giving, and loving others. No, He wants one gift, and that would be me, all of me. Then He can unwrap that gift and give Himself to others through me.

So my thought this year is: Have I wrapped myself in His love and what He gave me to use for His kingdom, or have I wrapped myself in beautiful wrappings and said, "Well, that is done for this year"?

Let's make this coming year a year that belongs to Him, knowing His heart for a lost world and caring enough to let Him be Himself in us and flow out to others. May each of us offer ourselves as a gift to Him all 365 days and make every day a special day to celebrate Him!

# Time to Huddle

As I began to pray about the New Year of 2009, I began to remember when my son played for a state championship basketball team. I thought of the many lessons I learned as a fan and supporter of the school, but most of all in the role of mother of one of the players. I can't tell you how many uniforms I washed, how many trips I made to pick up kids from practices, and how many meals I prepared each day because of late practices or games.

I thought back to the excitement that was there when we thought there was the possibility we could be state champs. This started when my son was in the sixth grade and my father took him to the state tournaments to watch Strasburg win that goal that year. From that time forward, he never went many places without a basketball in his hands. He dribbled up and down the streets to school, he played in the evenings at the local school with a pick-up game among his friends, and his dad set up hairs in the basement, where he learned to dribble round them.

His dream took what looked like a wrong turn when we moved from that school and his friends right before his freshmen year. But he never lost the dream. At the beginning of his sophomore year, a new coach came with the same dream and began to put together the team that could fulfill it.

I could write a book telling of all the things my son—and his mom—had to learn to be the winner. Some of those you could probably guess. There were the training rules: no girls during the basketball season, be in the house by 10 p.m., be at every practice with the right attitude, learn the basic skills of the game, no showing off with fancy dunks, dribbling, or passing, and no blaming the referee for your failure to win.

There are so many lessons I could share with you that I learned as he learned, but I want to focus on the one that he shared with me just today. I believe it is the lesson that the Body of Christ must learn for this day and time we live in: What does it mean to be a team (or could we say, a body)?

When I look at most of the Body of Christ today, I see individuals. Individual talents and individual opinions of how this game (of life) should be played. But the main lesson my son said he learned is what I want to bring forth today: we need to do everything as a team! What does it mean to do my part as member of a team (or "body")? We must learn to sit together, travel together, and play together. If I don't do my part individually as a part of the team, we don't win.

The hard thing to learn in training as a member of a team is that sometimes your part is laying aside your talent and what you think you know so that another team member's abilities can come forth. What if you know you have practiced and practiced to be a good shooter and have succeeded in this area? Are you willing to be put in the position on the team of passing the ball off to another player? Do you rejoice with the person on your team who got all the glory in the newspaper the next day because he made the basket, even if there's not one word about how you passed him the ball in a way that made it easy for him to score?

As I talked about all of this with my son today, he shared something I had never seen before. He gave me the secret of being a team: "Mom, we sweat together, we laughed together, we encouraged each other, we learned and did the basics while the hard spots took care of themselves, but the important thing is that we huddled together." What does that mean, and why could that be the most important thing if we want to be winners?

I think I get it and oh, how I pray that the Body of Christ gets it, too! It is in the huddle that arms go around each other. It is in the huddle that the coach encourages the players just to go out and do what they have practiced all week. (Doesn't this sound like David facing Goliath?). It is in the huddle that the team is closest to the confidence of knowing what's true. It is in the huddle they join together to face this team that has challenged their ranking, and it is in the huddle that the team cry comes forth as they leave the huddle to get on with the game. There are no distractions now, no wondering who is going to be the star of this game, no negative thoughts of failing as an individual. One thing is evident in the huddle: there's a job to do, and it takes all of us to do it, including the cheerleaders, the fans—and the mothers.

You see, when I started out, I so wanted him to do well and to stand out, but I had to let go of that mother instinct and instead want the whole team to succeed as a team, not as individuals. As I sat among the parents, I never heard one negative comment about who was doing what, whether it was a good thing or an error.

What has happened to the teaching that we need each other? What has happened to the teaching that when one hurts, we all hurt? What has happened to the teaching that the greatest love is to lay down my life for my brother or sister? What has happened to the teaching that I should esteem you more highly than myself?

We have a prize as a Body (or team) that Paul teaches we should be pressing toward—namely, the call of Christ Jesus (Philippians 3:14–15). Was it not His last prayer to the Father that we would become one and that the world would know we are His by our love for each other?

So I present my case to the Body of Christ. Is this your heart? Which is most important: being seen and known, or allowing Jesus to be seen in us? *It's time for the Body of Christ to huddle!*

## HOLY DAYS AND HOLIDAYS

# Frogs or Freedom?

As I was looking ahead to the new year and thinking of what I wanted to be diligent in doing, I came across a scripture in my daily devotions that has stayed in the forefront of my mind. It is Exodus 8:1–15. In this scripture Moses was telling Pharaoh to let God's people go or He would smite the land with frogs. He said they would be in their houses, in their bedrooms, even in their beds, and in their servant's houses, upon the people, in their ovens, and in their bread dough as it was being prepared.

Well, Moses told Aaron to stretch forth his rod over the ponds and streams, causing frogs to come up upon the land. Then Pharaoh's magicians did the same, and there must have been frogs everywhere, just as Moses had warned Pharaoh. So Pharaoh called for Moses and Aaron and asked that God would take away the frogs; then he would let God's people go.

Now the part that really ministered to me: Moses asked Pharaoh when he should ask God for the frogs to be removed. Pharaoh had been given the right to set the time of deliverance from the frogs, and he answered "tomorrow." At once my mind went into action. He could have answered "right now," but he chose to have the frogs hang around another day. Why would he do that?

But then I realized I was doing the same thing in waiting for January 1 to start doing the things I already knew I should be doing. Was I allowing "frogs" to stay in my life situations when all I had to do was choose today to get rid of them instead of tomorrow? Then I began to think of some of the Scriptures that talked about "today," such as 2 Corinthians 6:2, which says that "now is the day of salvation" (KJV)!

So I asked myself the question: Why would I wait on a certain date when my Father has given me the power to face the frogs in my life and say *today* is the day I will be obedient to You and get them out of my life? I have made many New Year's resolutions in the past and kept very few of them. I have put off many things until tomorrow that I could have done today and should have done today.

Therefore, when you hear His voice *today*, remember Hebrews 3:7–8 and "harden not your hearts" (KJV)!

*Thank You, Father, You also said Your mercies are new every day [Lamentations 3:23], which shows me again that You deal with the todays. So this year my New Year's resolution has already begun.* Today *is where I will live, for as the scripture says, "This is the day which*

*the Lord hath made; we will rejoice and be glad in it"*
*[Psalm 118:24 KJV]. And I will get rid of all the frogs*
today*!*

## Notes & Reflections

# About the Author

Born in 1936 in Uhrichsville, Ohio, and now living in Port
Washington, Shirley Henry is a mother of five, grandmother of
seven, and great-grandmother of twelve. She was married to her
husband, Jim, for nearly 45 years, during which the Lord showed
her how His Word works. She is a servant of God and a follower of
Jesus, and is devoted to teaching others just how much He loves
them.

# About Believer To Book

Believer To Book believes your story should be touching lives, not hiding in your heart. Our process is simple:

**1)** We interview you to hear and outline your story.

**2)** We develop your story into a beautifully packaged book.

**3)** From publication to author platform, we take care of everything.

**Who We Are:** We are an extremely focused team of interviewers, writers, editors, designers, and new generation marketers.

**What We Do:** We help busy Christians turn their knowledge and stories into books—then position them for success in the marketplace.

**What Makes Us Special:** We offer a best-selling publishing experience that requires almost 0 touch after the initial interviews.

Learn more at believertobook.com.

62465687R10116

Made in the USA
Charleston, SC
15 October 2016